MYTHOLOGY GRAPHICS

THE CURSE OF MEDUSA

A MODERN GRAPHIC GREEK MYTH

BY JESSICA GUNDERSON

ILLUSTRATED BY MARIAN SLOANE

CAPSTONE PRESS

a capstone imprint

Published by Capstone Press, an imprint of Capstone
1710 Roe Crest Drive, North Mankato, Minnesota 56003
capstonepub.com

Library of Congress Cataloging-in-Publication Data is available
on the Library of Congress website.

ISBN: 9781669059097 (hardcover)
ISBN: 9781669059172 (paperback)
ISBN: 9781669059189 (ebook PDF)

Summary: Life isn't easy when you're cursed with a head of snakes for hair.
Medusa knows that better than anyone. But she didn't start out in such a state.
What happened? Who's to blame? And who's the real hero? Find out in this modern,
action-packed graphic retelling of a classic Greek myth.

Editorial Credits
Editor: Alison Deering; Designer: Jaime Willems; Production Specialist:
Whitney Schaefer

Printed and bound in the USA. PO 5626

TABLE OF CONTENTS

CHAPTER 1

WARRIOR DREAMS

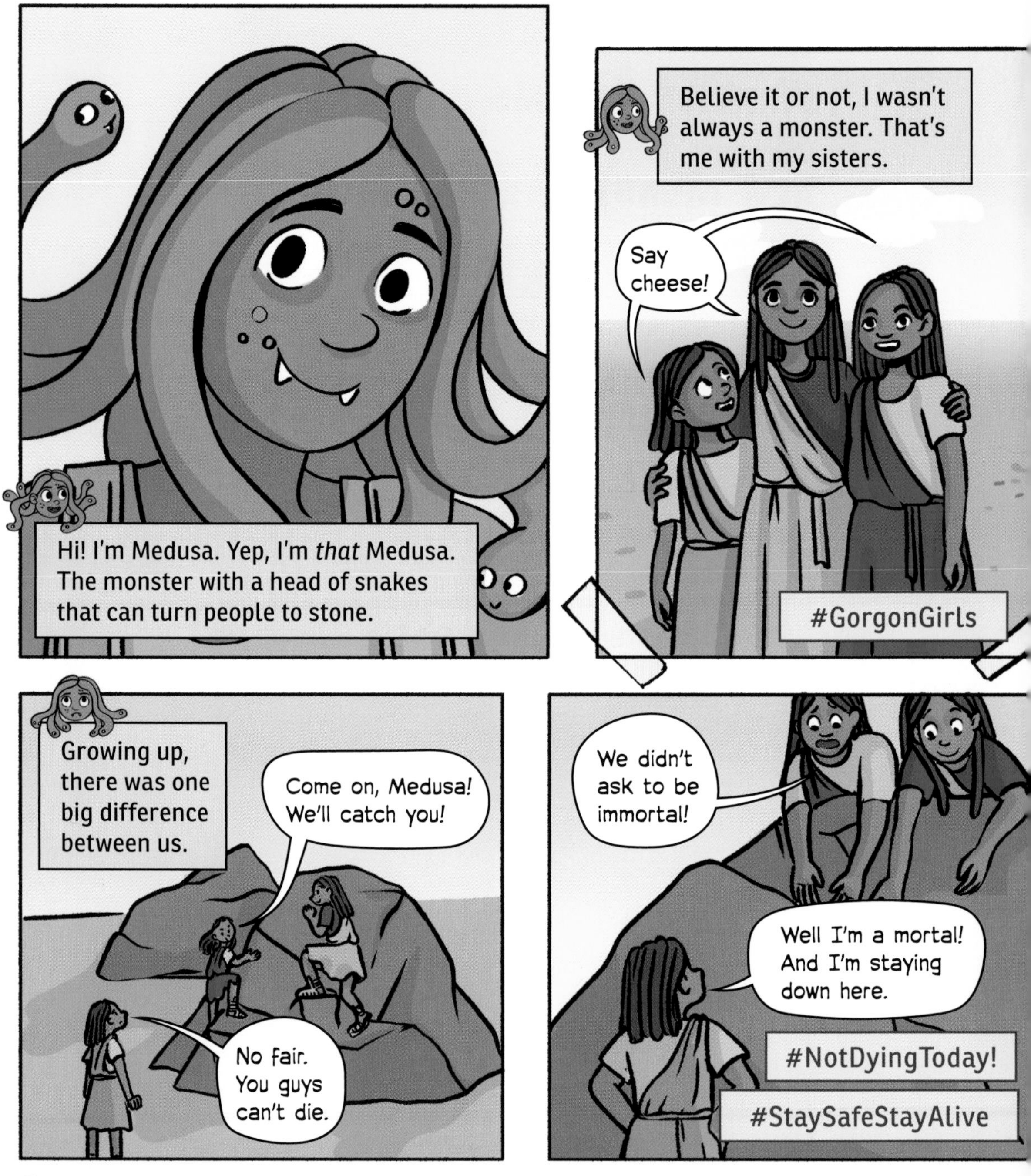

Hi! I'm Medusa. Yep, I'm *that* Medusa. The monster with a head of snakes that can turn people to stone.
Believe it or not, I wasn't always a monster. That's me with my sisters.
Say cheese!
#GorgonGirls
Growing up, there was one big difference between us.
Come on, Medusa! We'll catch you!
No fair. You guys can't die.
We didn't ask to be immortal!
Well I'm a mortal! And I'm staying down here.
#NotDyingToday!
#StaySafeStayAlive

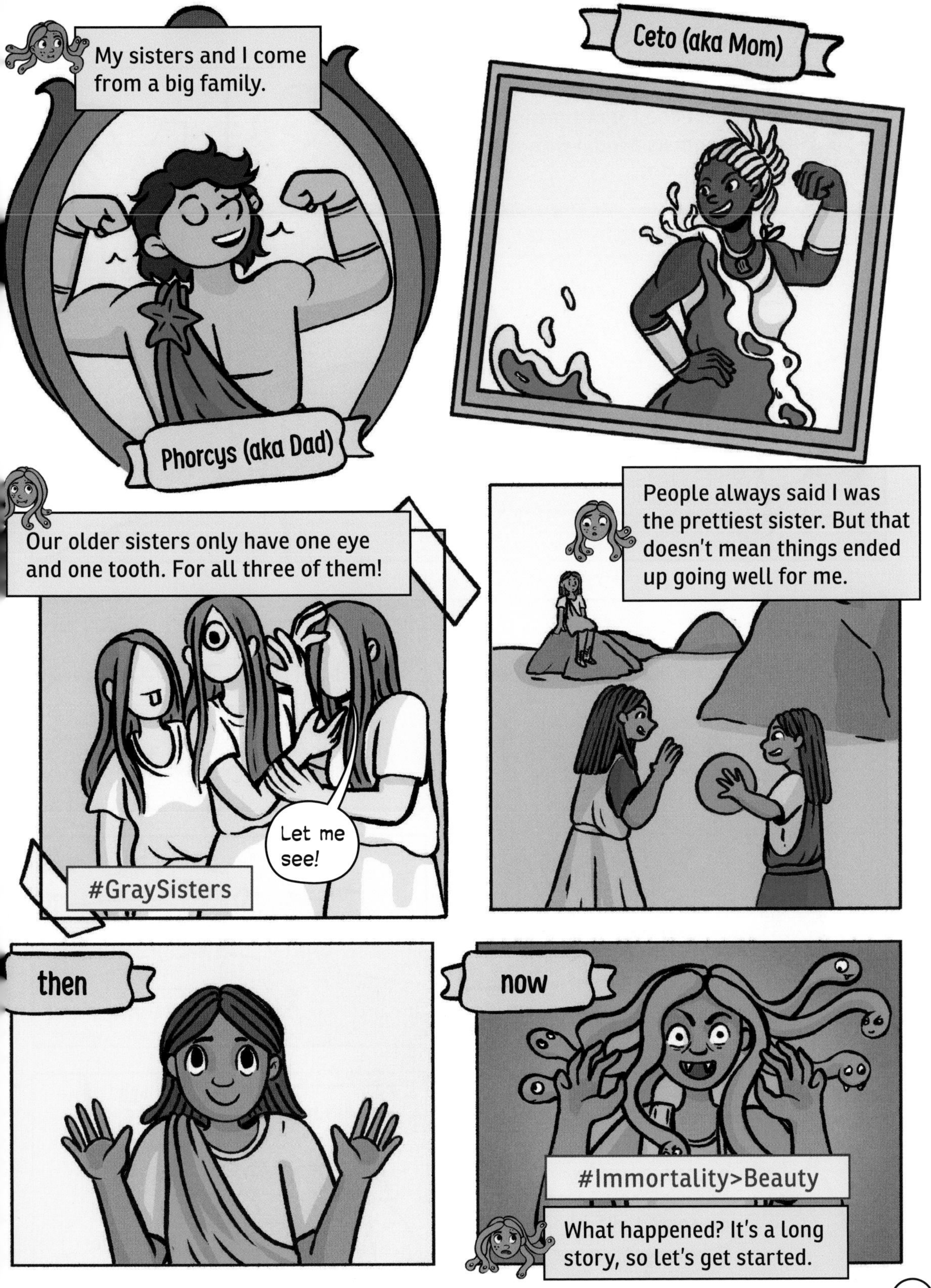
My sisters and I come from a big family.
Phorcys (aka Dad)
Ceto (aka Mom)
Our older sisters only have one eye and one tooth. For all three of them!
Let me see!
#GraySisters
People always said I was the prettiest sister. But that doesn't mean things ended up going well for me.
then
now
#Immortality>Beauty
What happened? It's a long story, so let's get started.

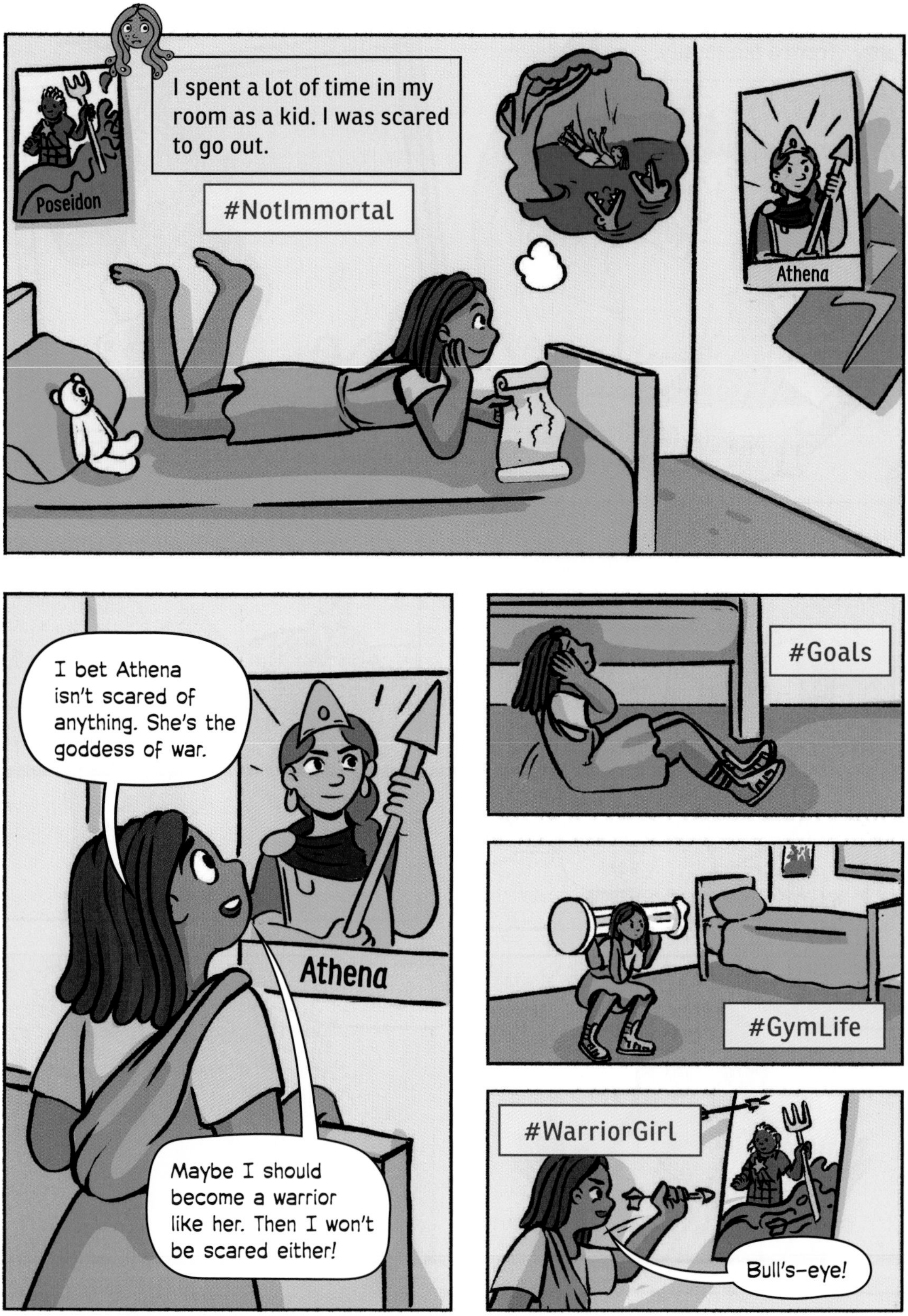
Poseidon
I spent a lot of time in my room as a kid. I was scared to go out.
#NotImmortal
Athena
I bet Athena isn't scared of anything. She's the goddess of war.
Athena
Maybe I should become a warrior like her. Then I won't be scared either!
#Goals
#GymLife
#WarriorGirl
Bull's-eye!

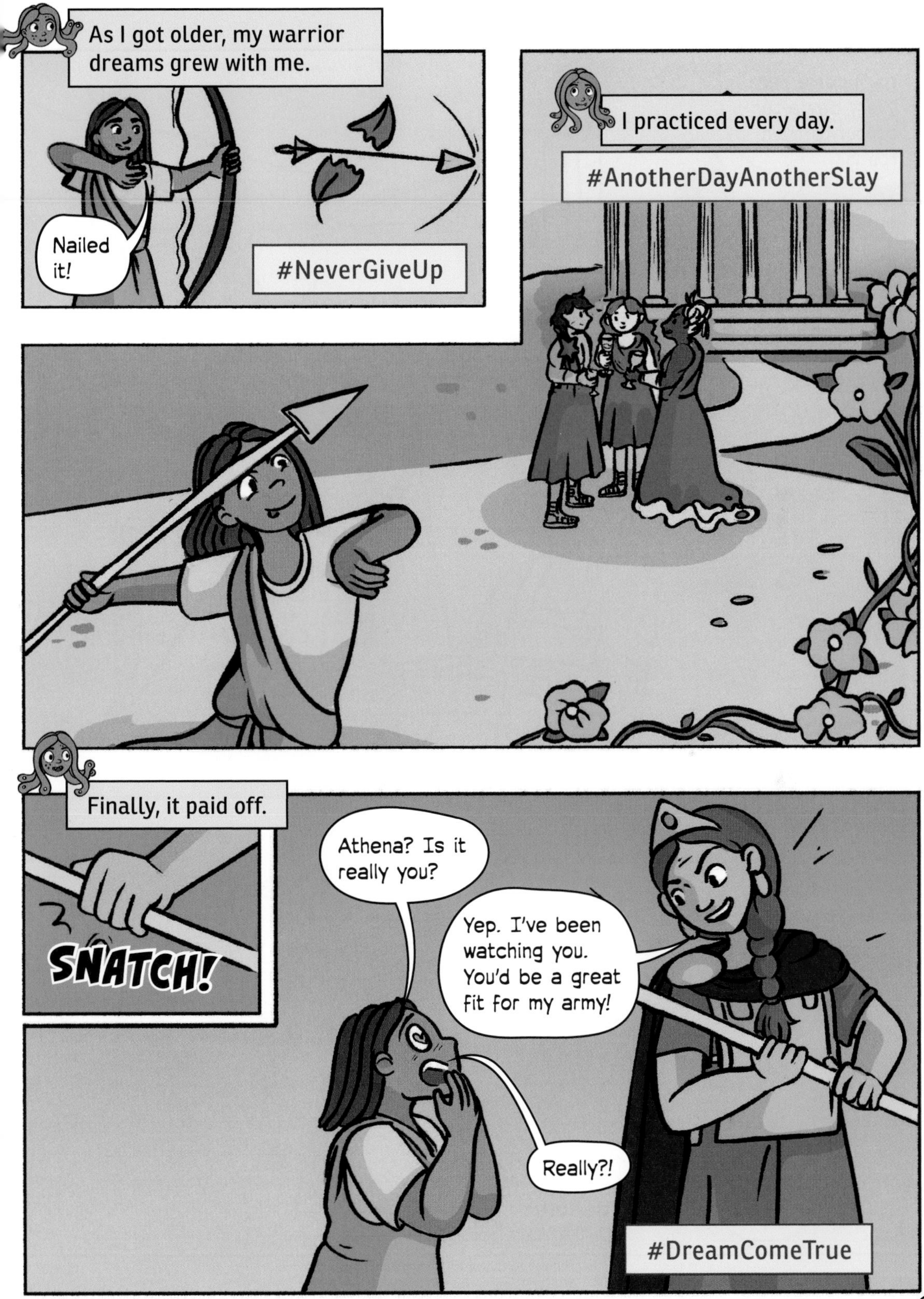

As I got older, my warrior dreams grew with me.
Nailed it!
#NeverGiveUp
I practiced every day.
#AnotherDayAnotherSlay
Finally, it paid off.
SNATCH!
Athena? Is it really you?
Yep. I've been watching you. You'd be a great fit for my army!
Really?!
#DreamComeTrue

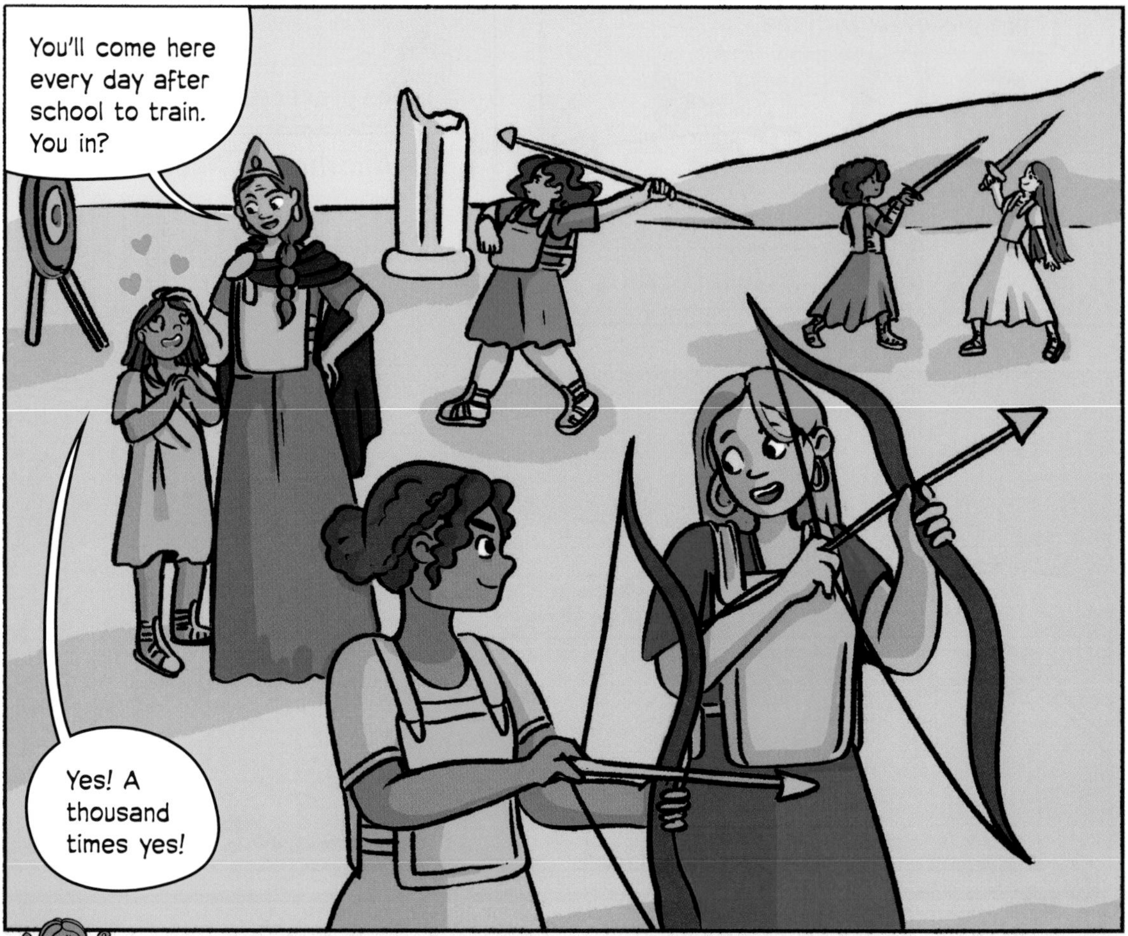
You'll come here every day after school to train. You in?
Yes! A thousand times yes!

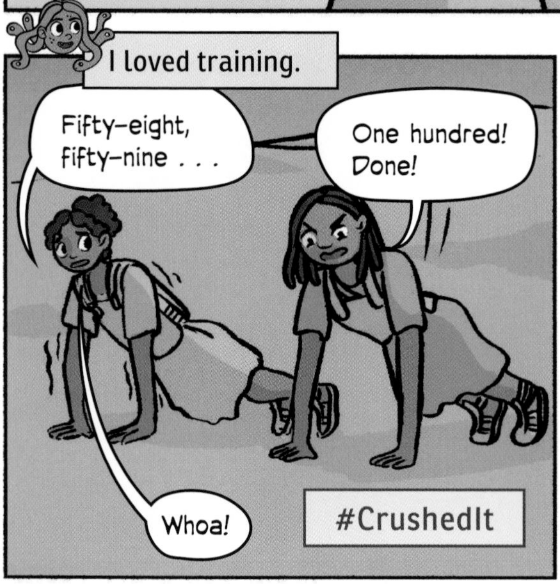
I loved training.
Fifty-eight, fifty-nine . . .
One hundred! Done!
Whoa!
#CrushedIt

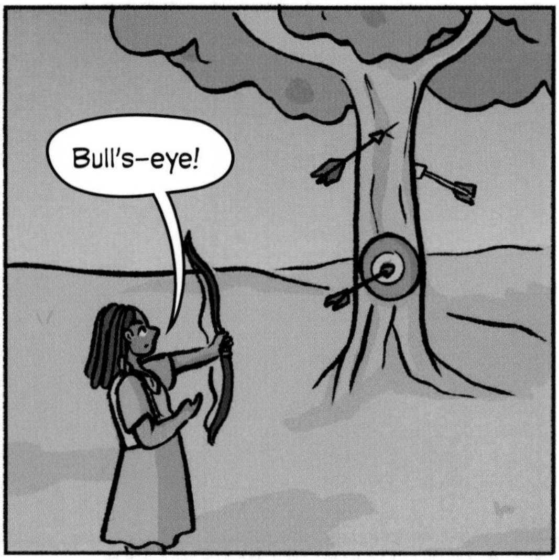
Bull's-eye!

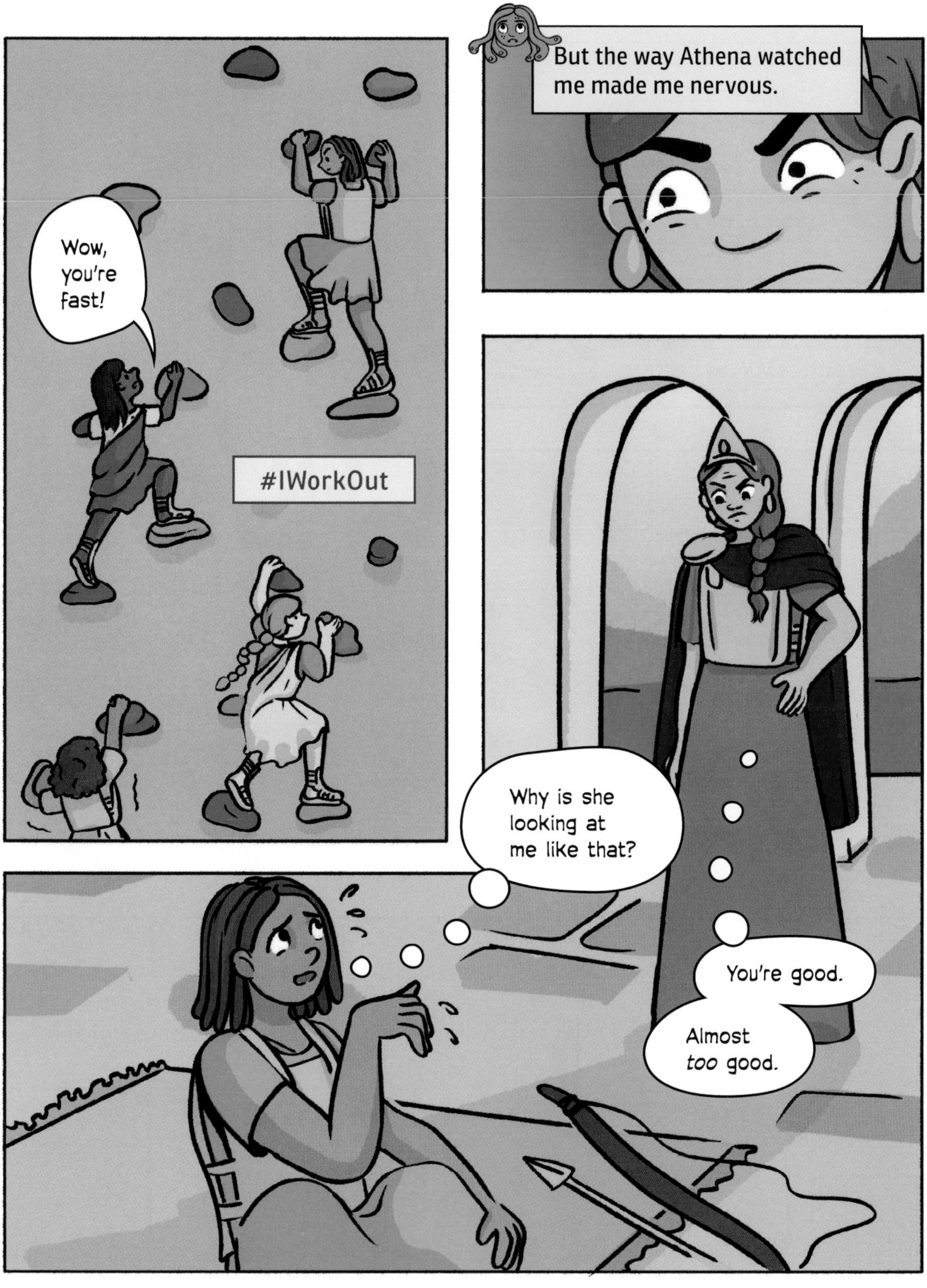
Wow, you're fast!
#IWorkOut
But the way Athena watched me made me nervous.
Why is she looking at me like that?
You're good.
Almost *too* good.

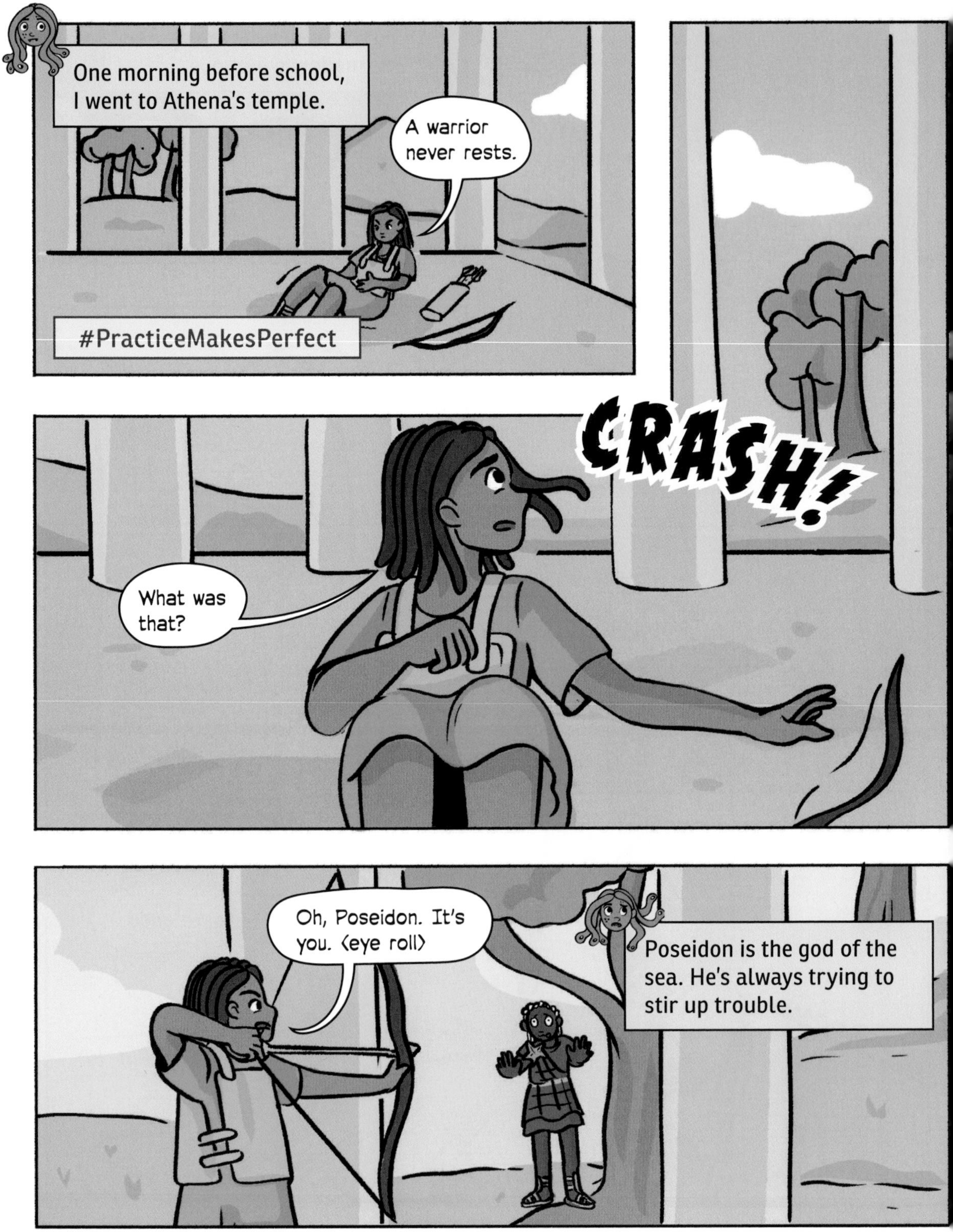
One morning before school, I went to Athena's temple.
A warrior never rests.
#PracticeMakesPerfect
CRASH!
What was that?
Oh, Poseidon. It's you. <eye roll>
Poseidon is the god of the sea. He's always trying to stir up trouble.

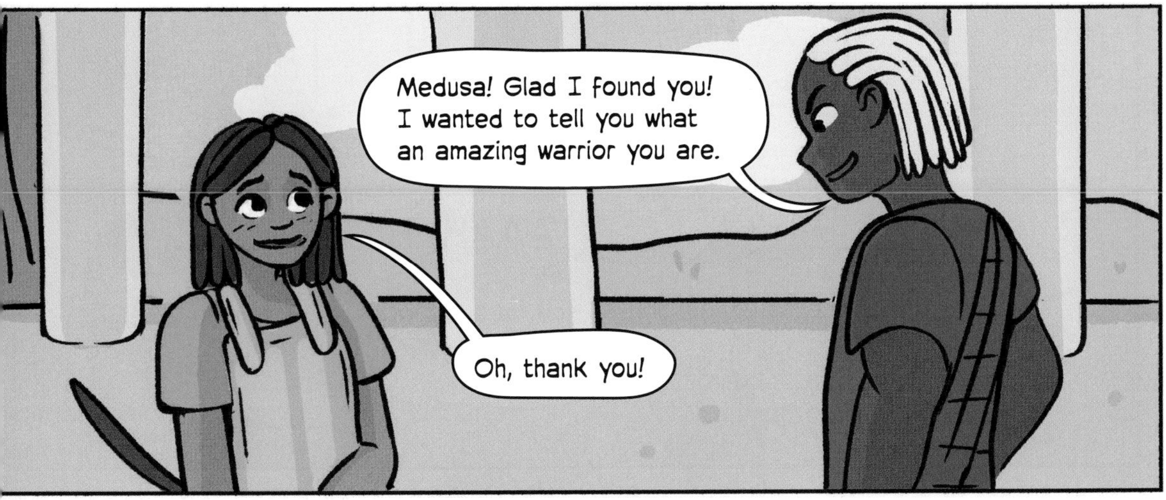
Medusa! Glad I found you! I wanted to tell you what an amazing warrior you are.
Oh, thank you!

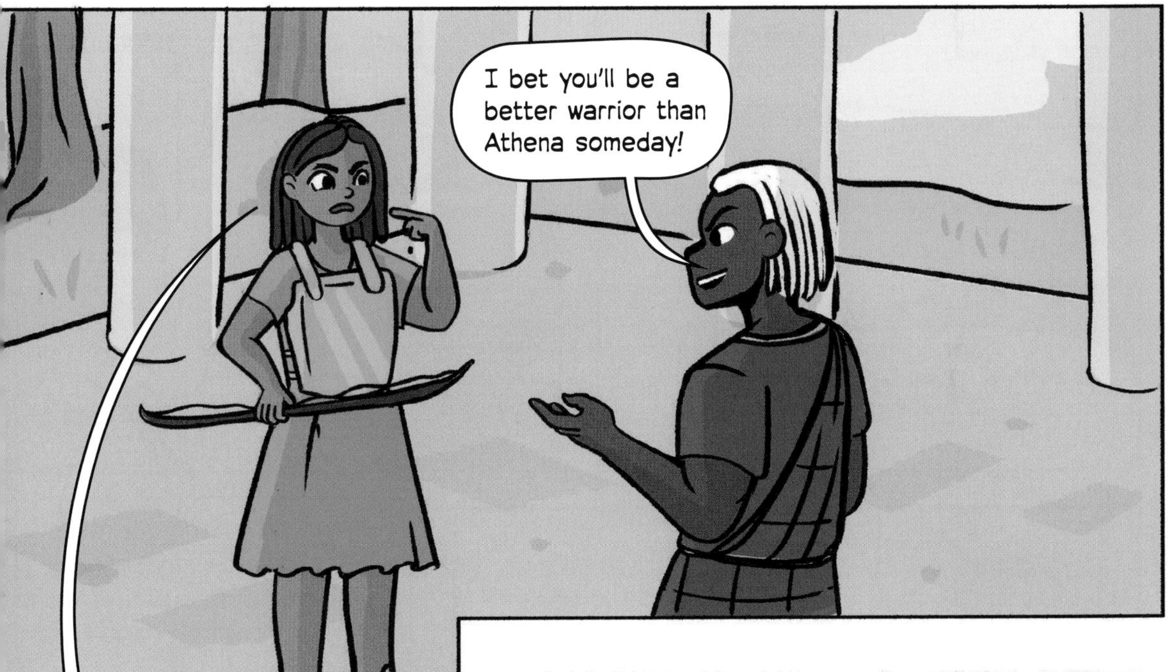
I bet you'll be a better warrior than Athena someday!
Someday? I'm already WAYYY better!

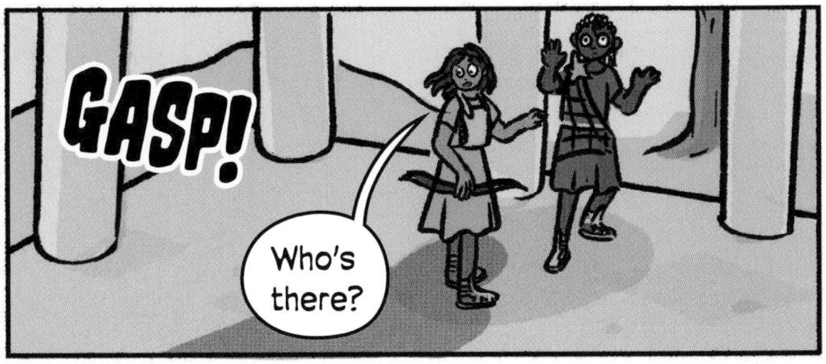
GASP!
Who's there?

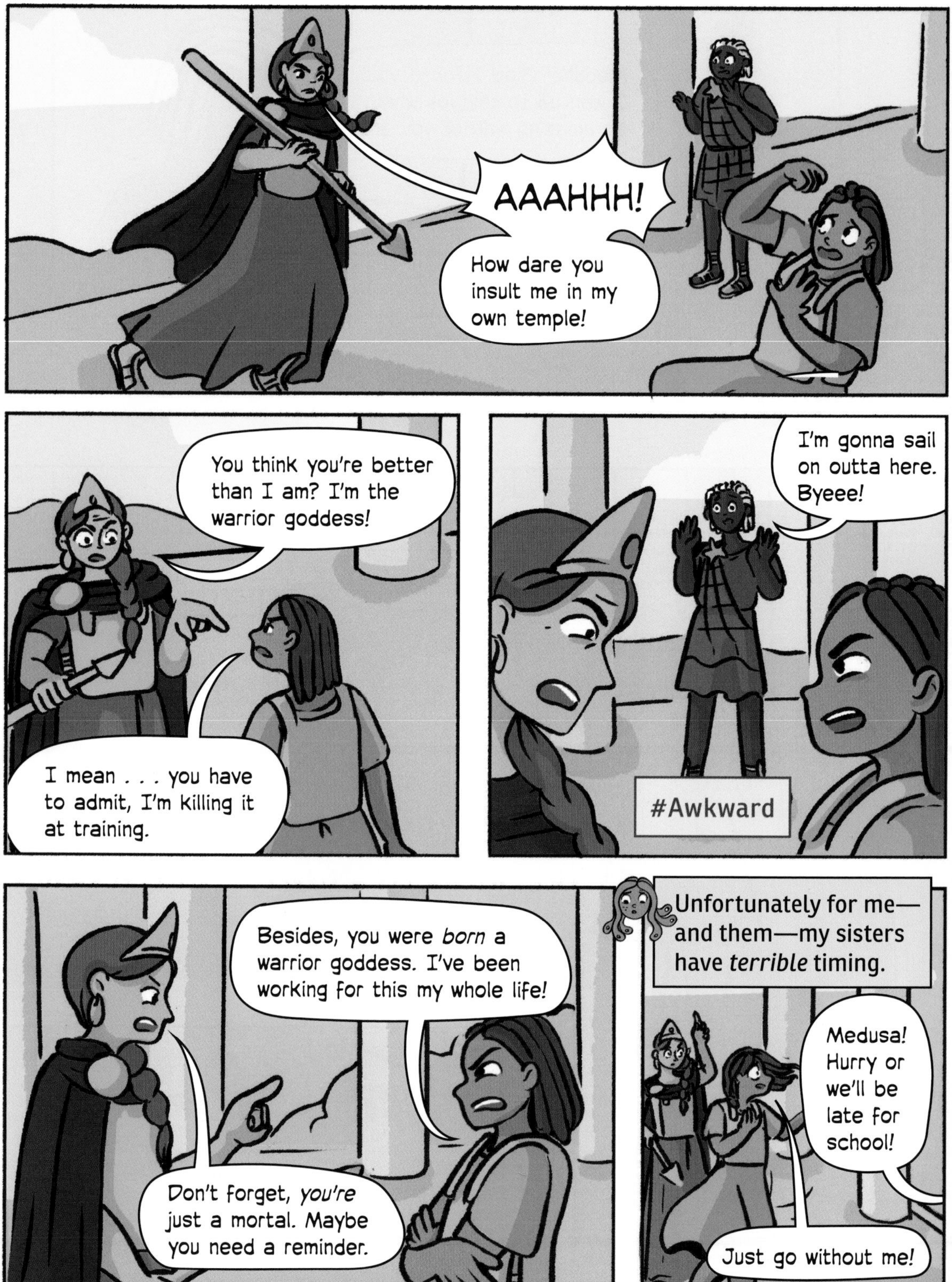
AAAHHH!
How dare you insult me in my own temple!
You think you're better than I am? I'm the warrior goddess!
I mean . . . you have to admit, I'm killing it at training.
I'm gonna sail on outta here. Byeee!
#Awkward
Besides, you were *born* a warrior goddess. I've been working for this my whole life!
Don't forget, *you're* just a mortal. Maybe you need a reminder.
Unfortunately for me—and them—my sisters have *terrible* timing.
Medusa! Hurry or we'll be late for school!
Just go without me!

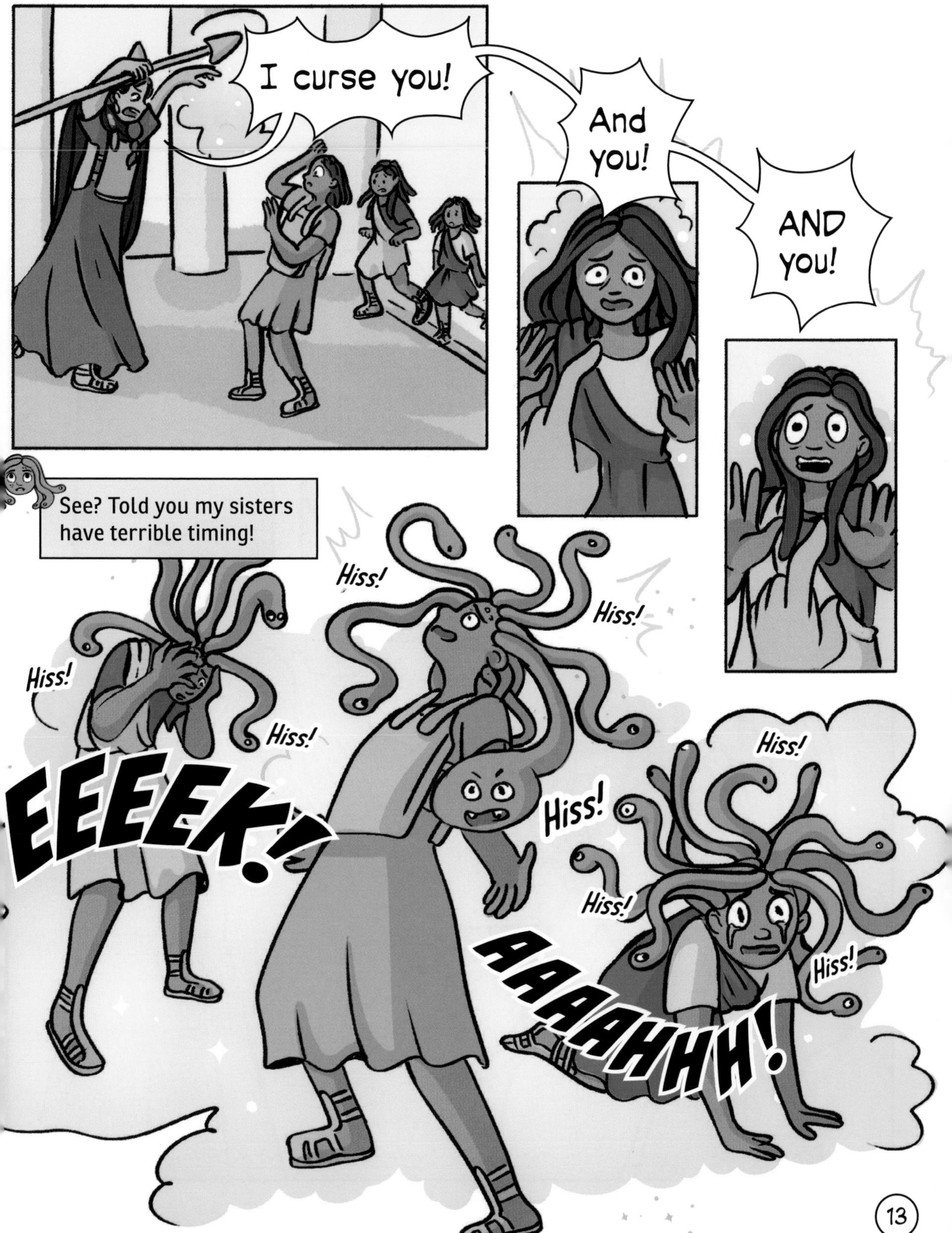
I curse you!
And you!
AND you!
See? Told you my sisters have terrible timing!
Hiss!
Hiss!
Hiss!
Hiss!
EEEEK!
Hiss!
Hiss!
Hiss!
AAAAHHHH!
Hiss!

CHAPTER 2

NEW MONSTER, NEW ME

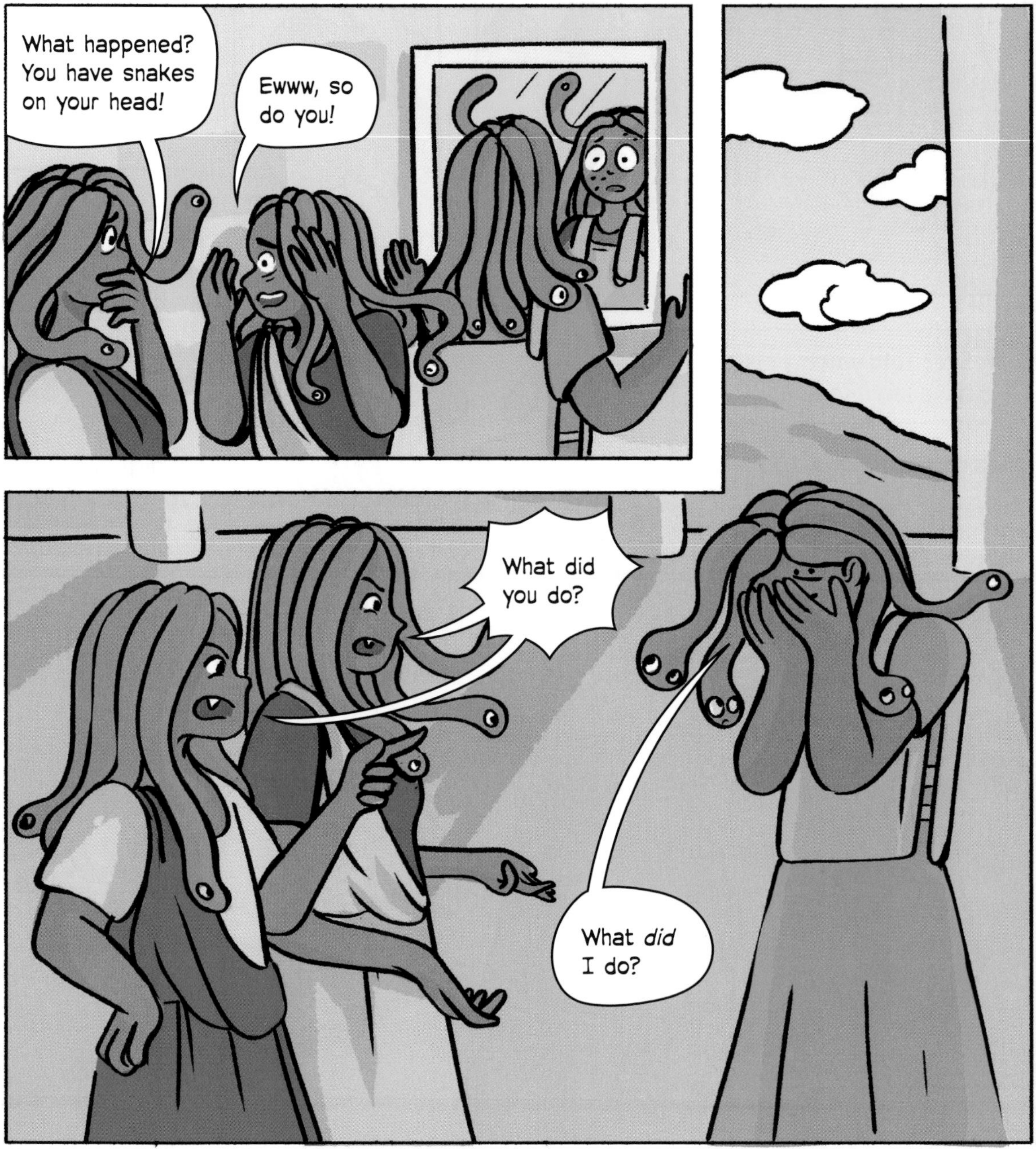
What happened? You have snakes on your head!
Ewww, so do you!
What did you do?
What *did* I do?

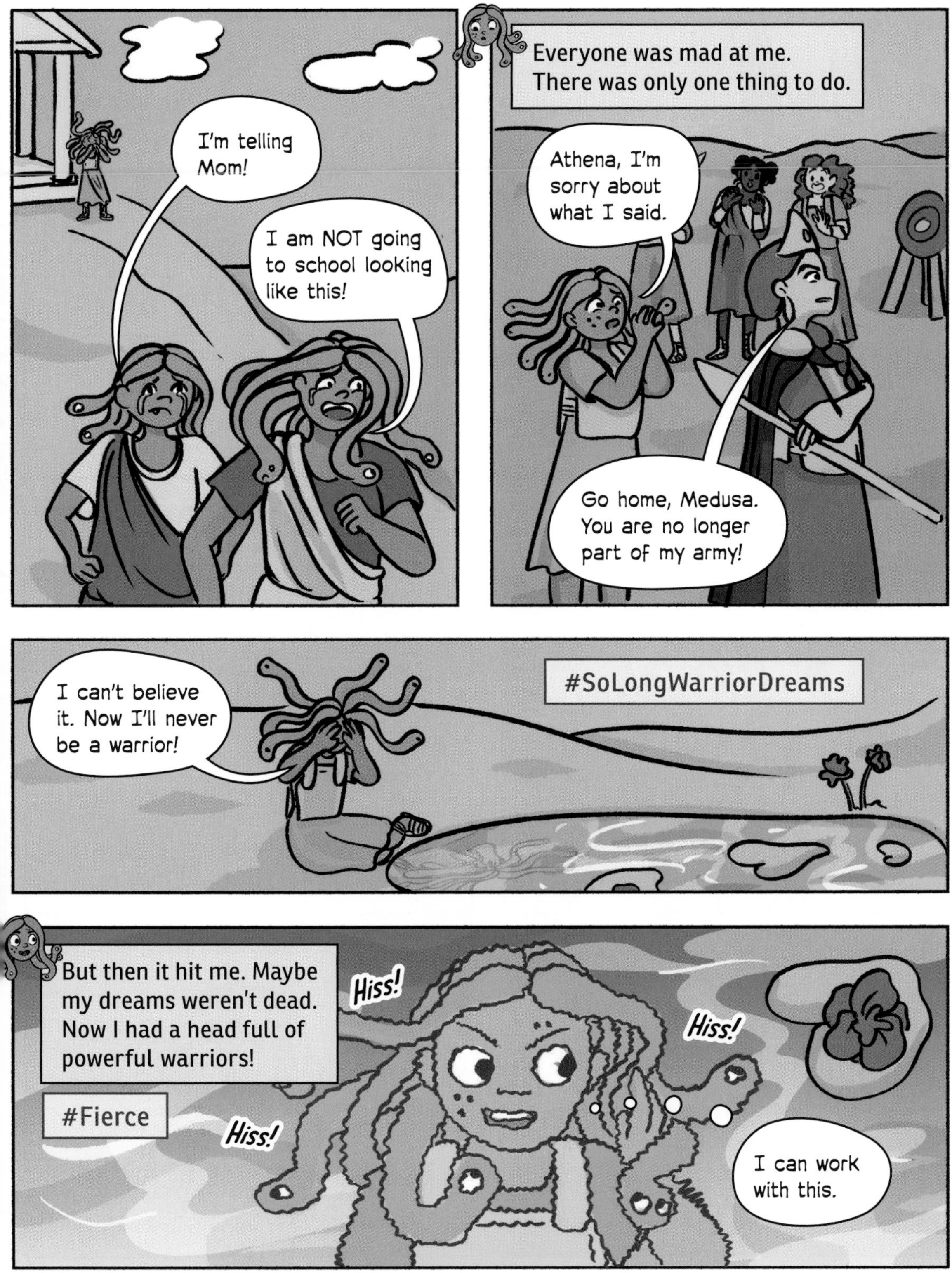

I'm telling Mom!
I am NOT going to school looking like this!
Everyone was mad at me. There was only one thing to do.
Athena, I'm sorry about what I said.
Go home, Medusa. You are no longer part of my army!
I can't believe it. Now I'll never be a warrior!
#SoLongWarriorDreams
But then it hit me. Maybe my dreams weren't dead. Now I had a head full of powerful warriors!
#Fierce
Hiss!
Hiss!
Hiss!
I can work with this.

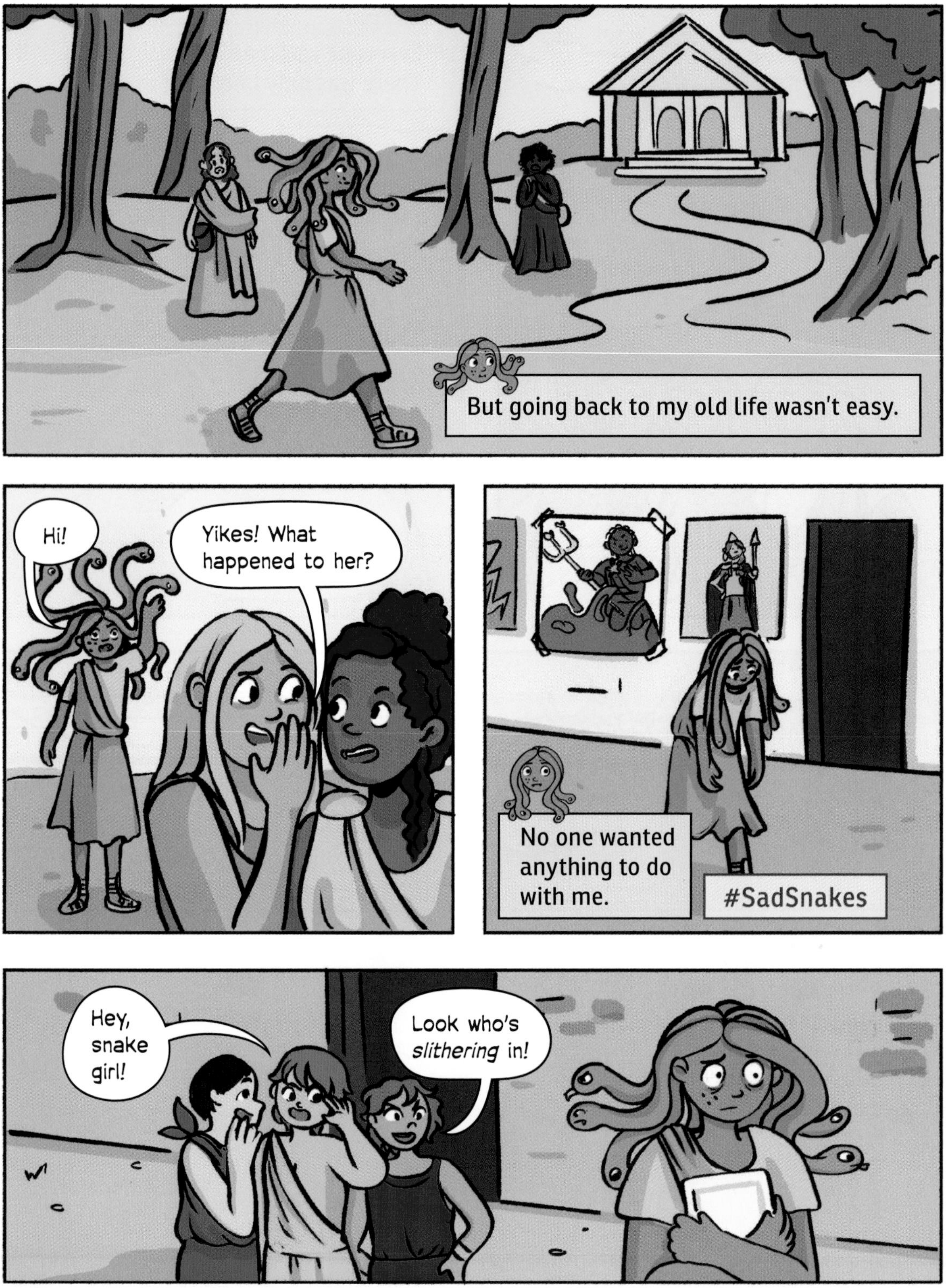
But going back to my old life wasn't easy.
Hi!
Yikes! What happened to her?
No one wanted anything to do with me.
#SadSnakes
Hey, snake girl!
Look who's *slithering* in!

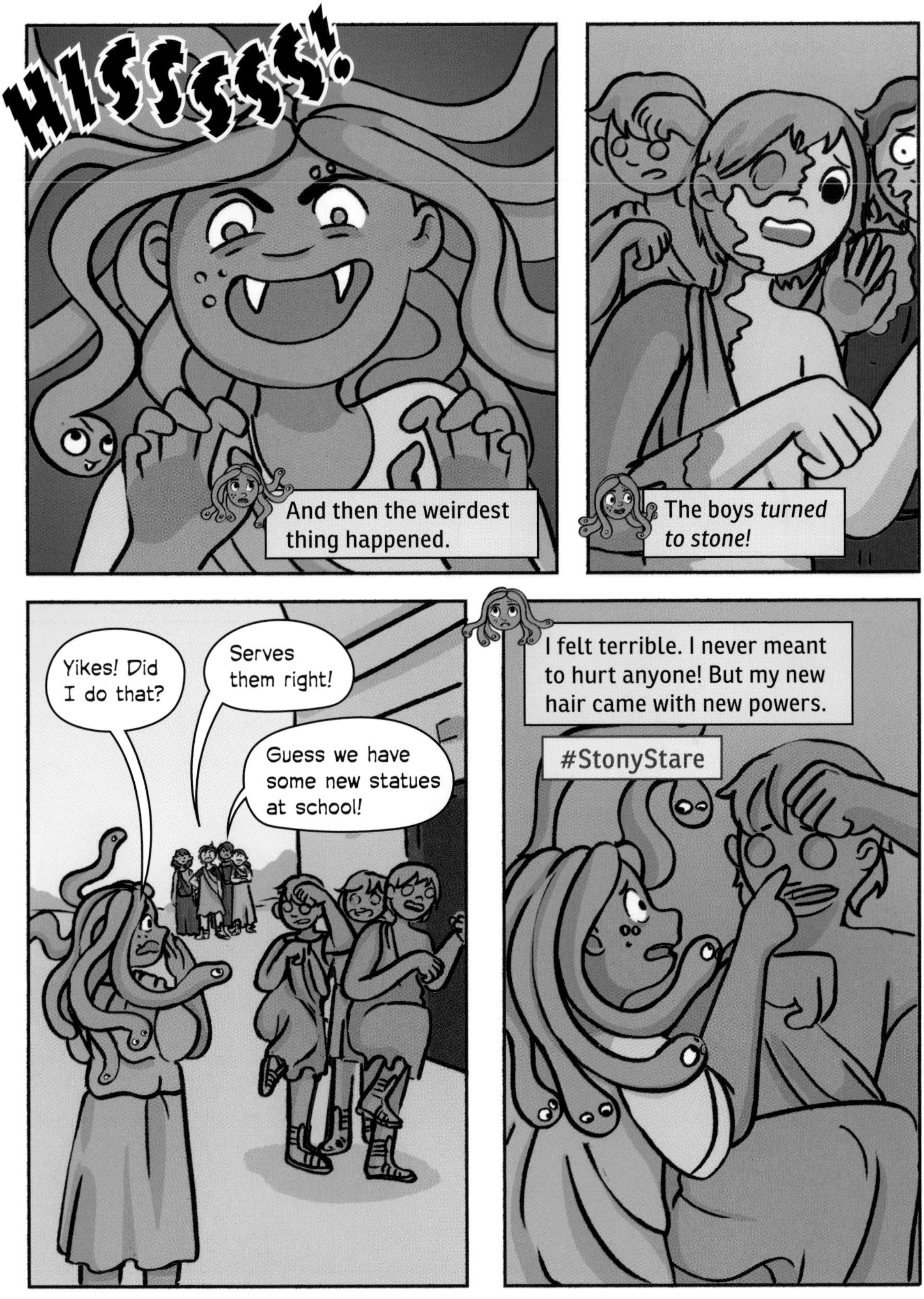
HISSSSS!
And then the weirdest thing happened.
The boys *turned to stone!*
Yikes! Did I do that?
Serves them right!
Guess we have some new statues at school!
I felt terrible. I never meant to hurt anyone! But my new hair came with new powers.
#StonyStare

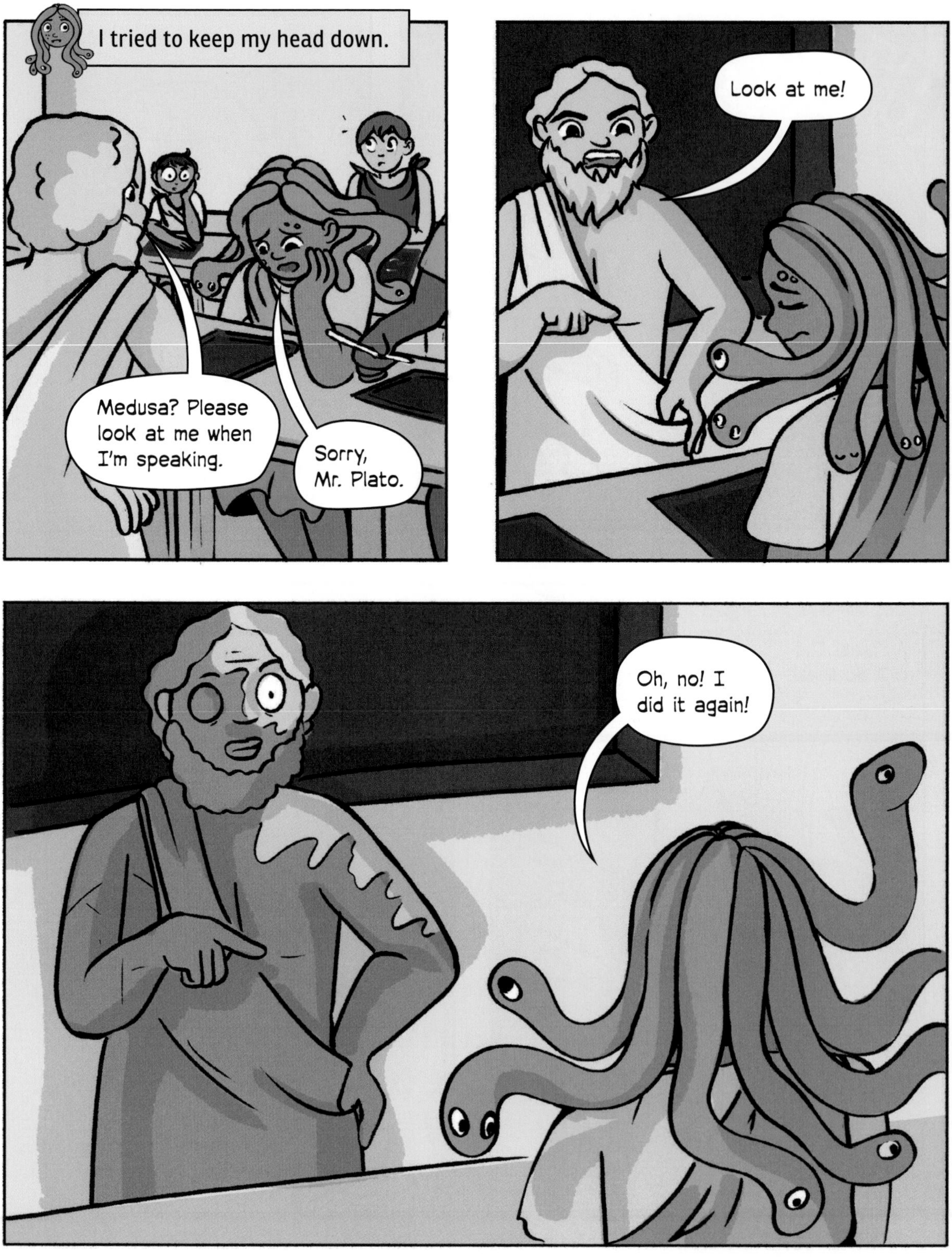
I tried to keep my head down.
Medusa? Please look at me when I'm speaking.
Sorry, Mr. Plato.
Look at me!
Oh, no! I did it again!

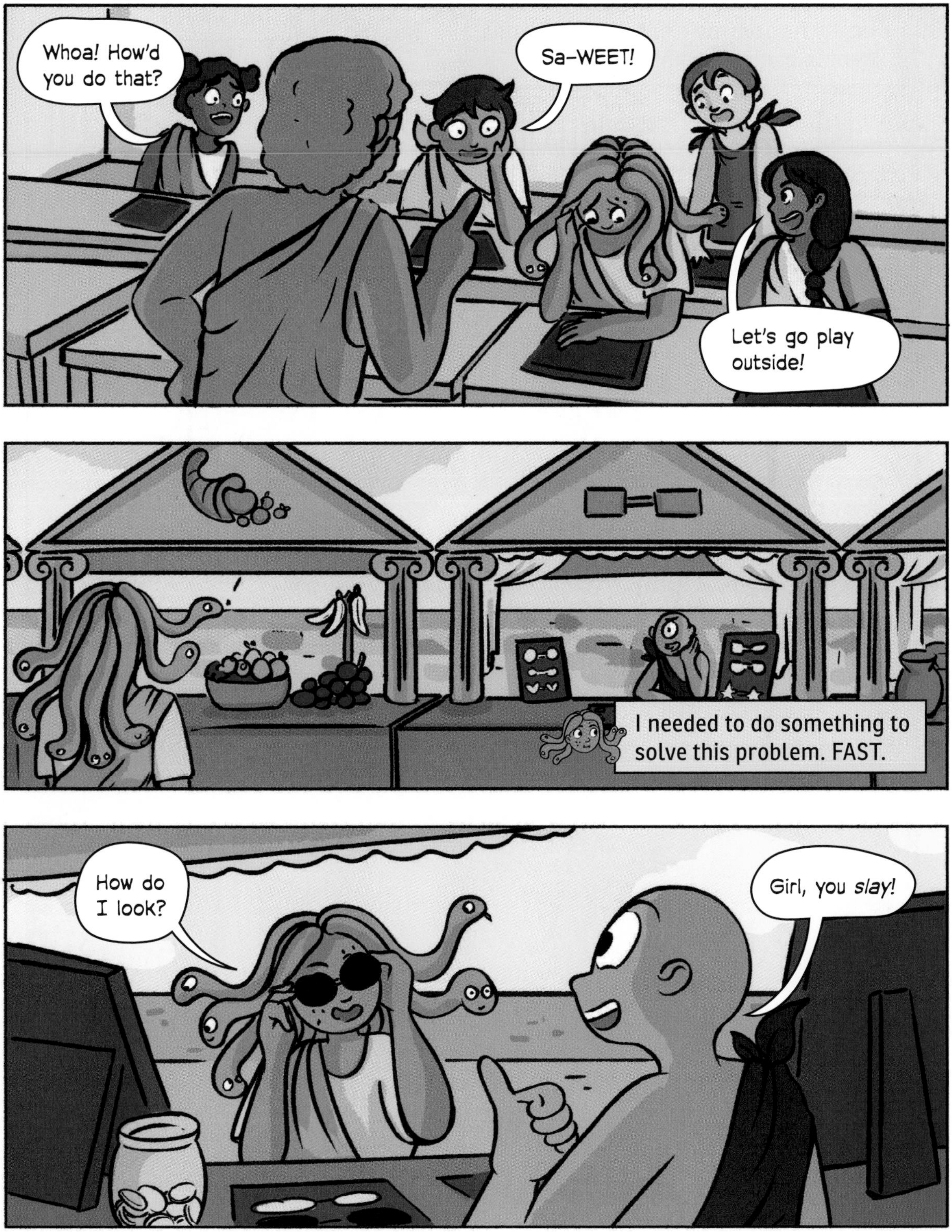
Whoa! How'd you do that?
Sa-WEET!
Let's go play outside!
I needed to do something to solve this problem. FAST.
How do I look?
Girl, you *slay*!

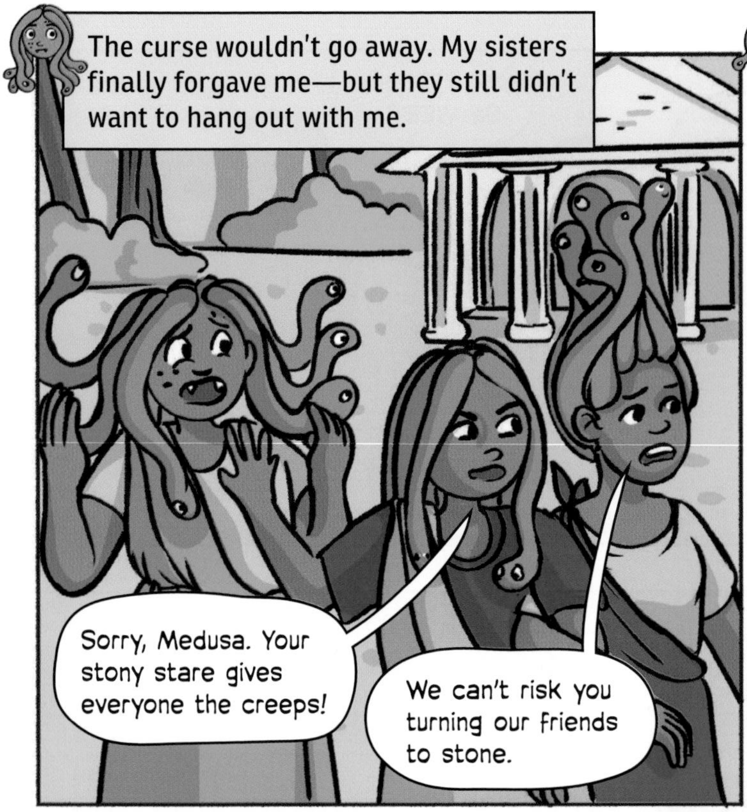
The curse wouldn't go away. My sisters finally forgave me—but they still didn't want to hang out with me.
Sorry, Medusa. Your stony stare gives everyone the creeps!
We can't risk you turning our friends to stone.

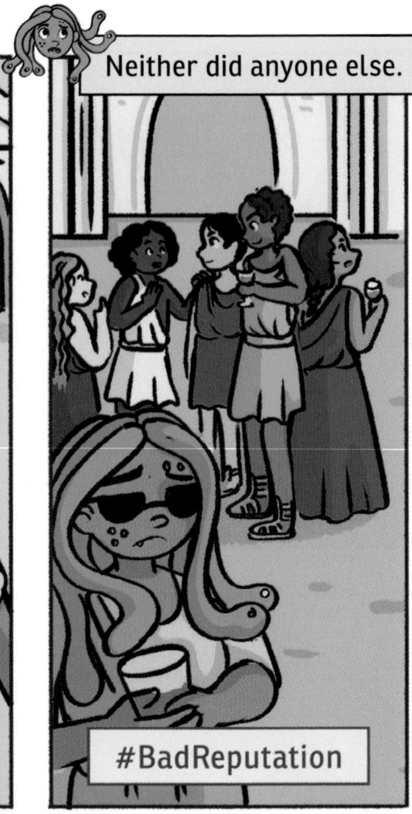
Neither did anyone else.
#BadReputation

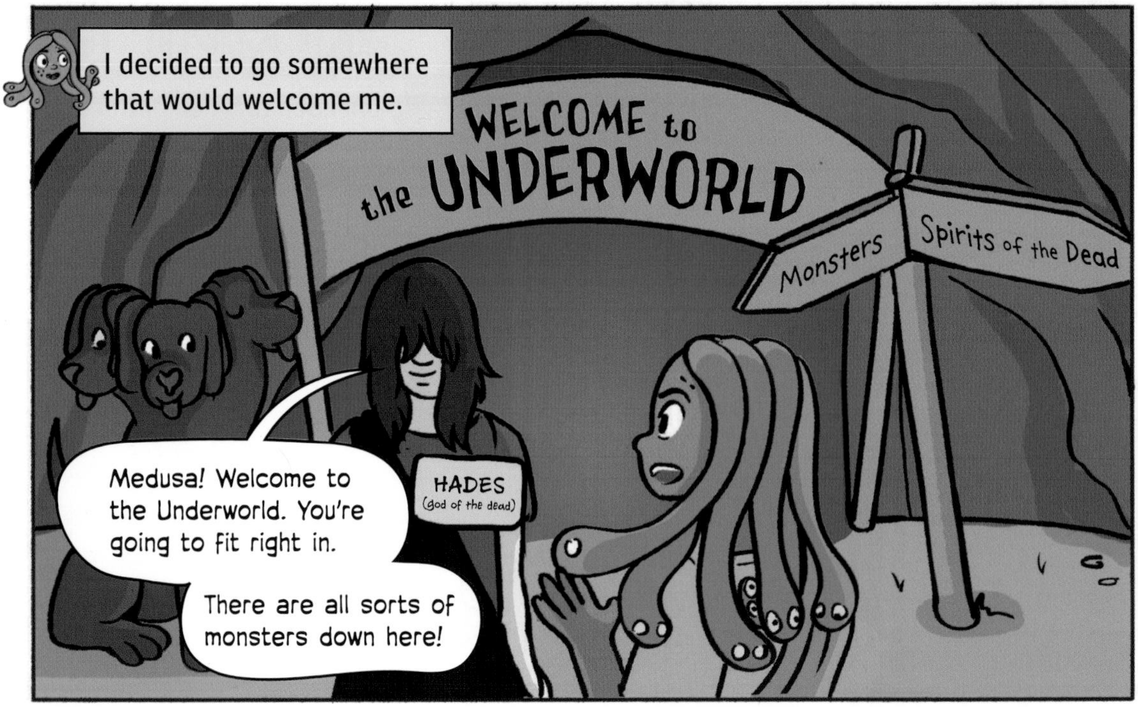
I decided to go somewhere that would welcome me.
WELCOME to the UNDERWORLD
Monsters
Spirits of the Dead
Medusa! Welcome to the Underworld. You're going to fit right in.
HADES (god of the dead)
There are all sorts of monsters down here!

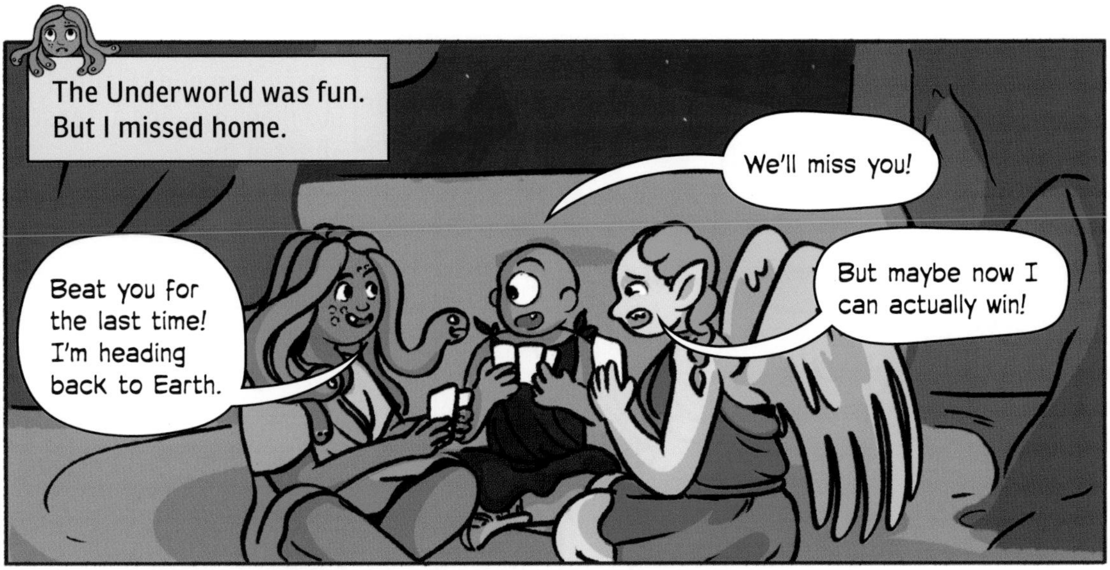
The Underworld was fun. But I missed home.
Beat you for the last time! I'm heading back to Earth.
We'll miss you!
But maybe now I can actually win!

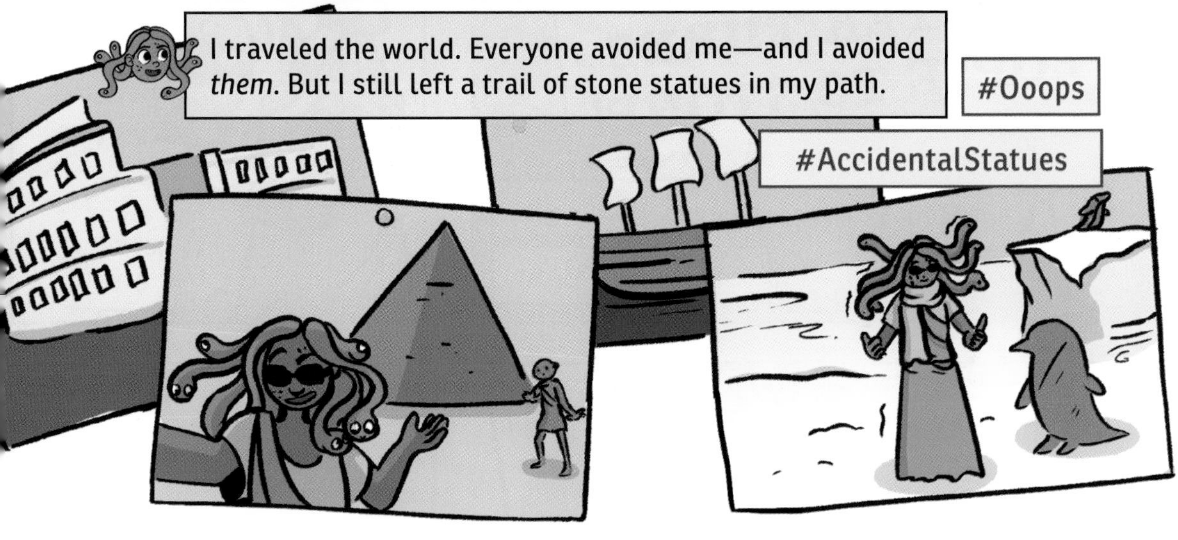
I traveled the world. Everyone avoided me—and I avoided *them*. But I still left a trail of stone statues in my path.
#Ooops
#AccidentalStatues

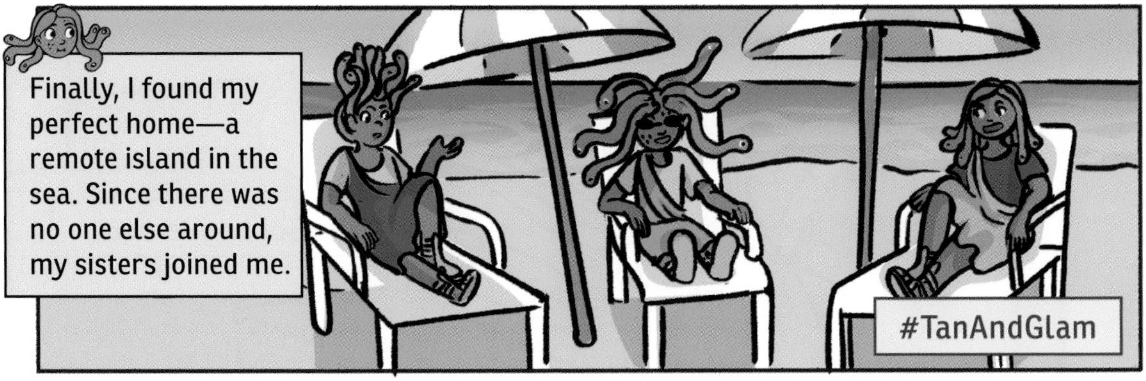
Finally, I found my perfect home—a remote island in the sea. Since there was no one else around, my sisters joined me.
#TanAndGlam

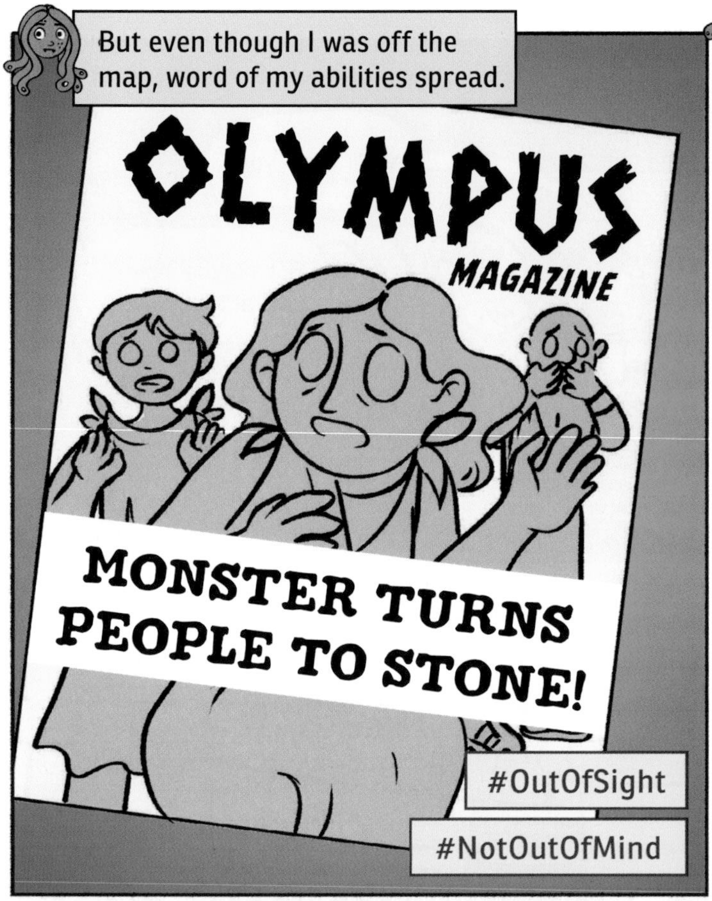
But even though I was off the map, word of my abilities spread.
OLYMPUS
MAGAZINE
MONSTER TURNS PEOPLE TO STONE!
#OutOfSight
#NotOutOfMind

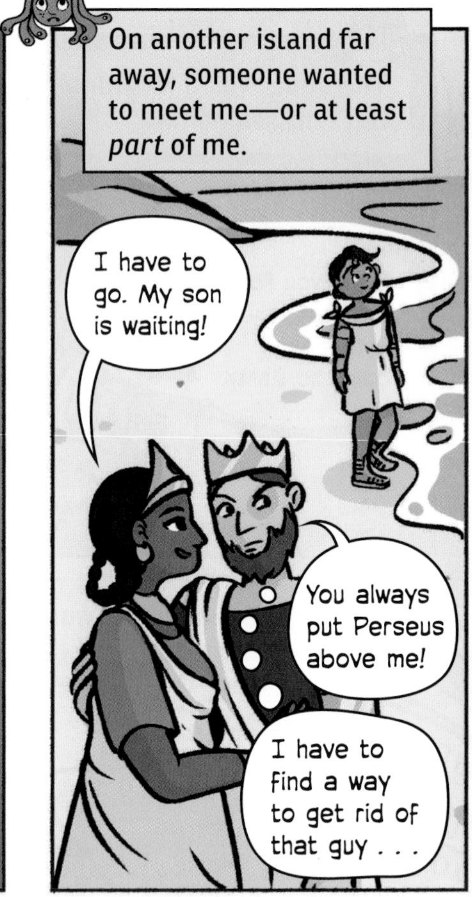
On another island far away, someone wanted to meet me—or at least *part* of me.
I have to go. My son is waiting!
You always put Perseus above me!
I have to find a way to get rid of that guy . . .

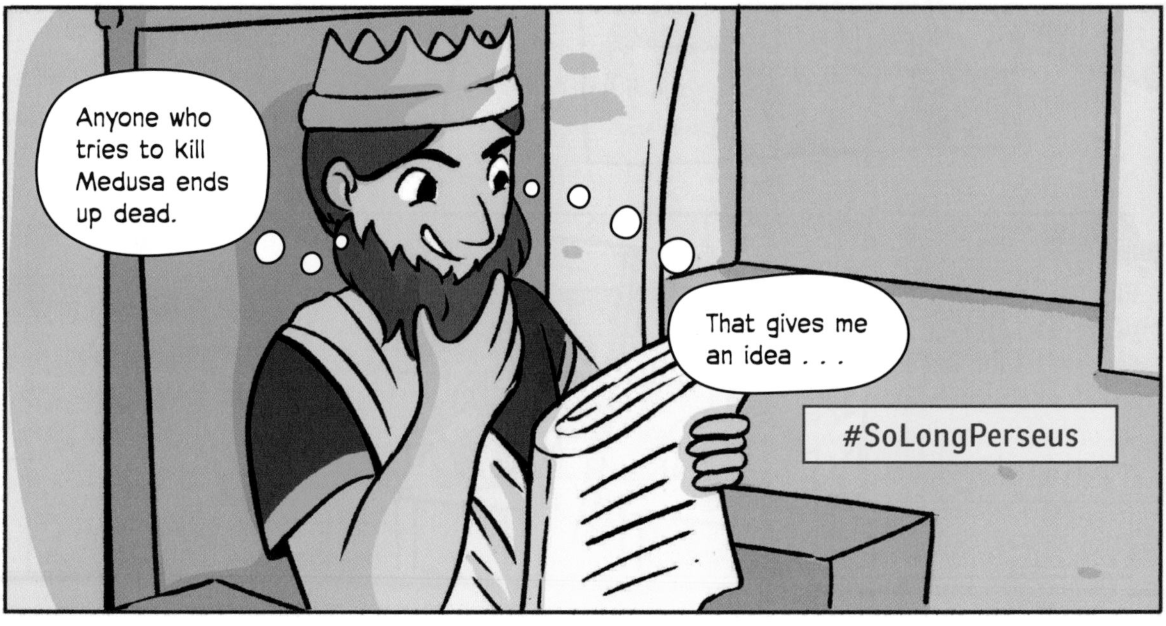
Anyone who tries to kill Medusa ends up dead.
That gives me an idea . . .
#SoLongPerseus

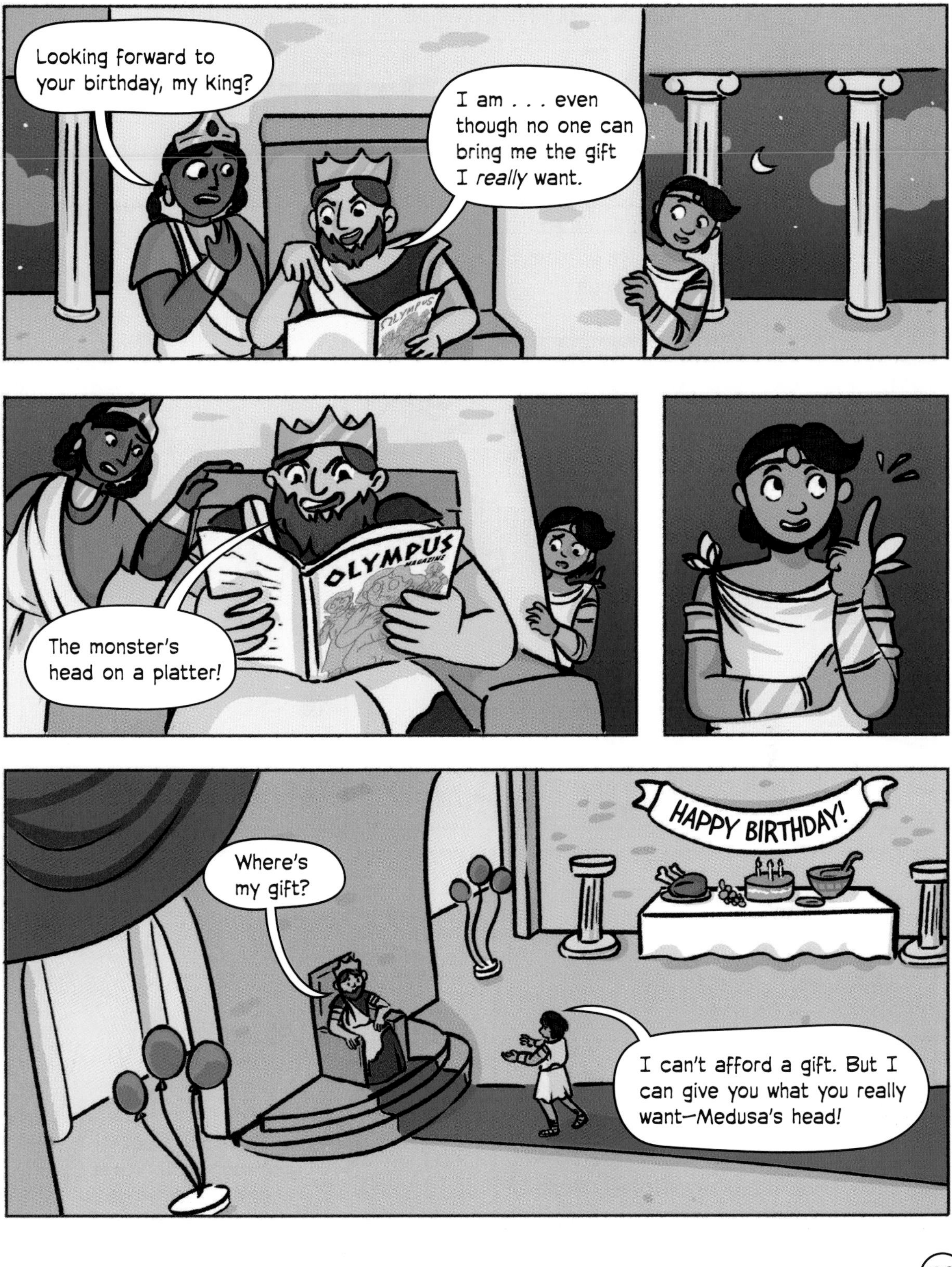
Looking forward to your birthday, my king?
I am . . . even though no one can bring me the gift I *really* want.
The monster's head on a platter!
OLYMPUS
HAPPY BIRTHDAY!
Where's my gift?
I can't afford a gift. But I can give you what you really want—Medusa's head!

CHAPTER 3

A QUEST BEGINS

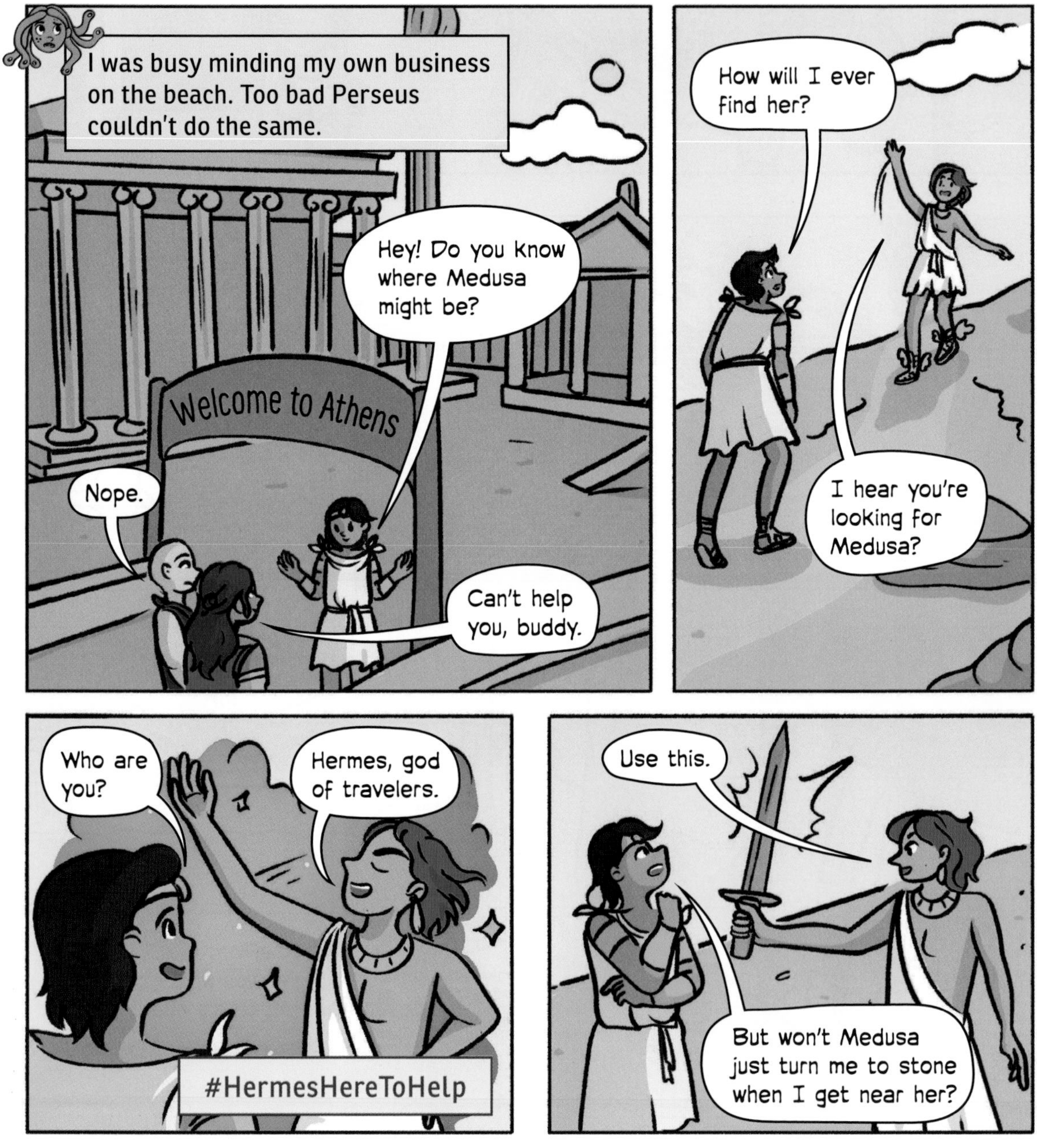
I was busy minding my own business on the beach. Too bad Perseus couldn't do the same.
Hey! Do you know where Medusa might be?
Welcome to Athens
Nope.
Can't help you, buddy.
How will I ever find her?
I hear you're looking for Medusa?
Who are you?
Hermes, god of travelers.
#HermesHereToHelp
Use this.
But won't Medusa just turn me to stone when I get near her?

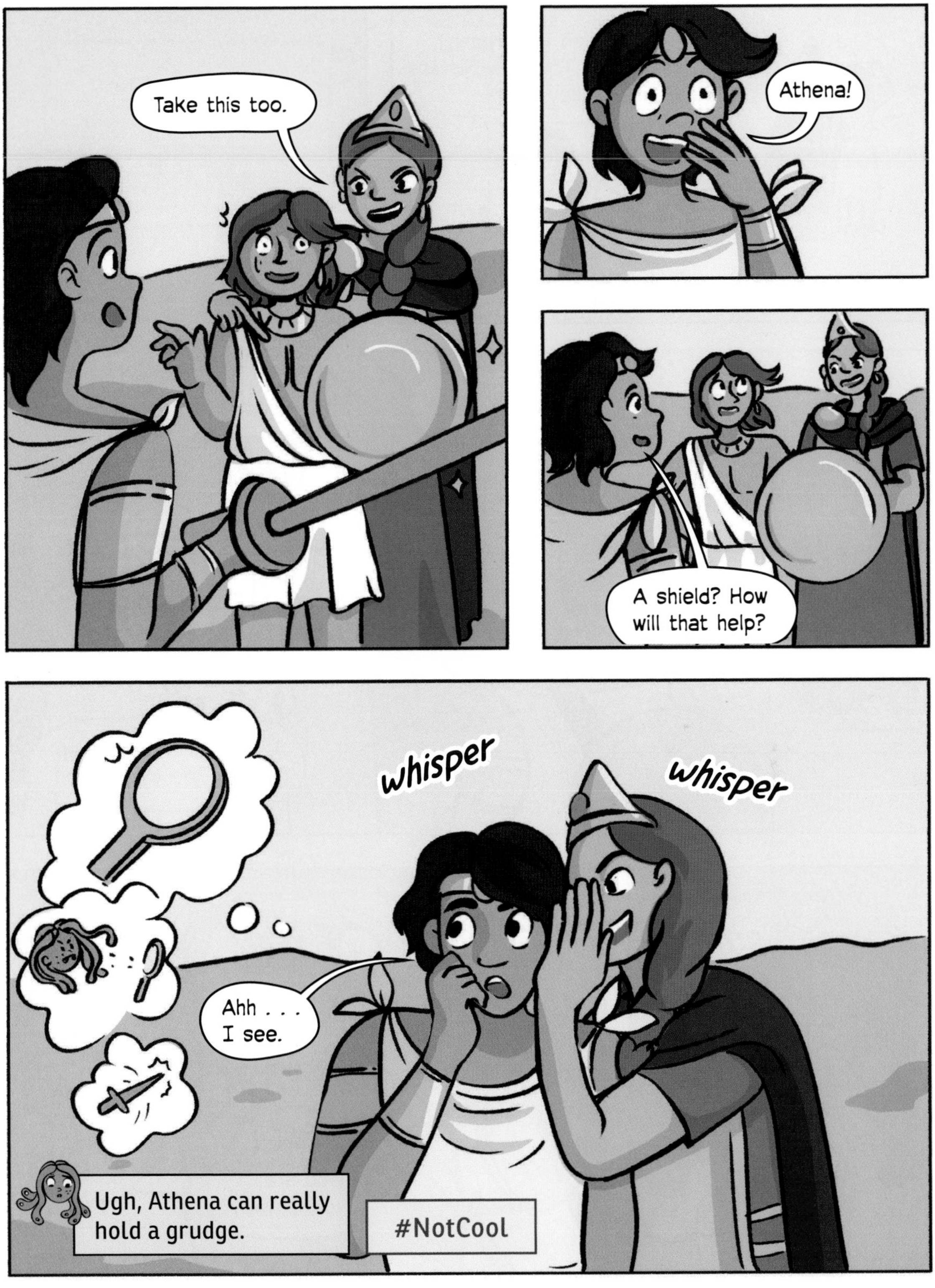
Take this too.
Athena!
A shield? How will that help?
whisper
whisper
Ahh . . . I see.
Ugh, Athena can really hold a grudge.
#NotCool

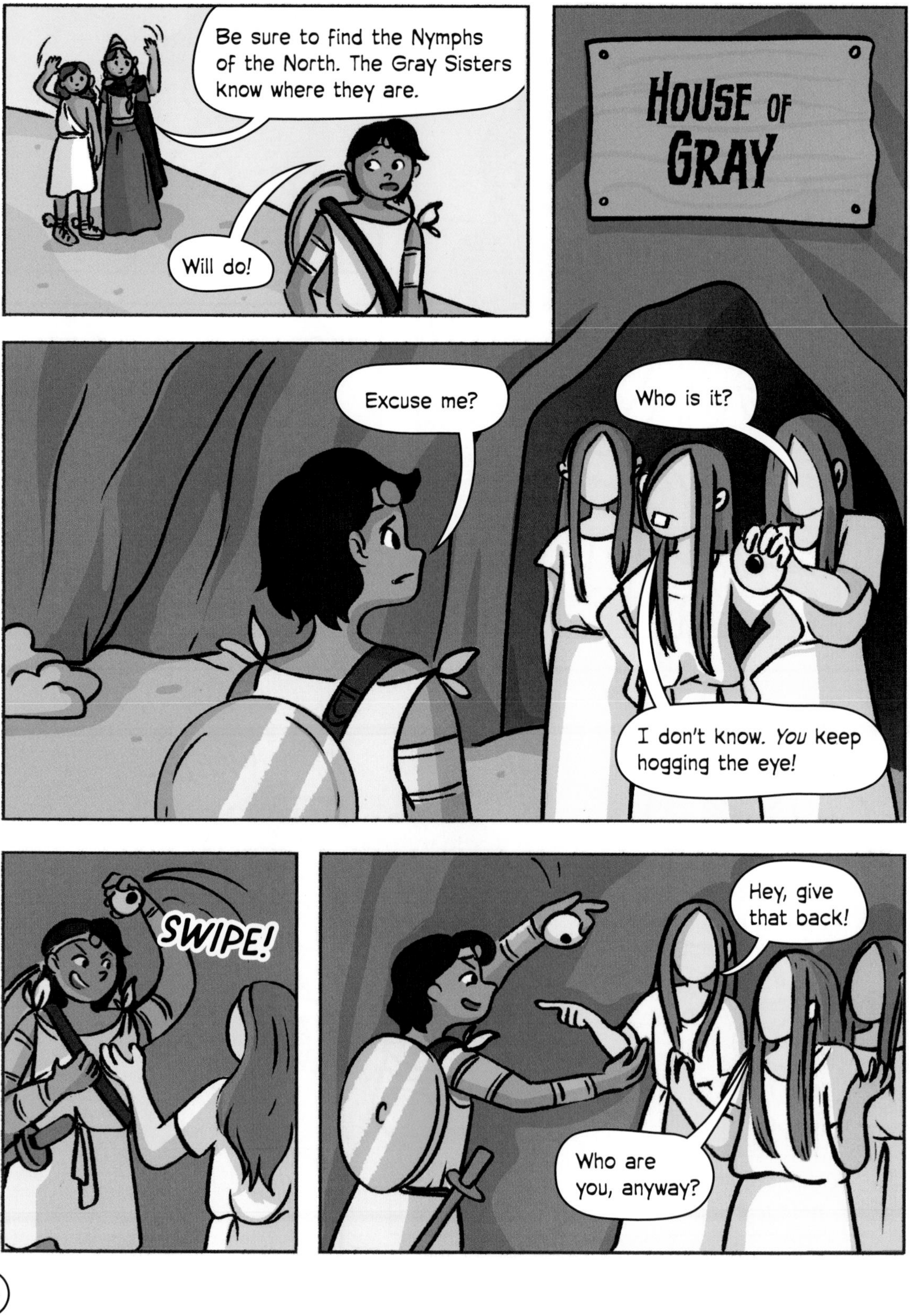
Be sure to find the Nymphs of the North. The Gray Sisters know where they are.
Will do!
HOUSE OF GRAY
Excuse me?
Who is it?
I don't know. *You* keep hogging the eye!
SWIPE!
Hey, give that back!
Who are you, anyway?

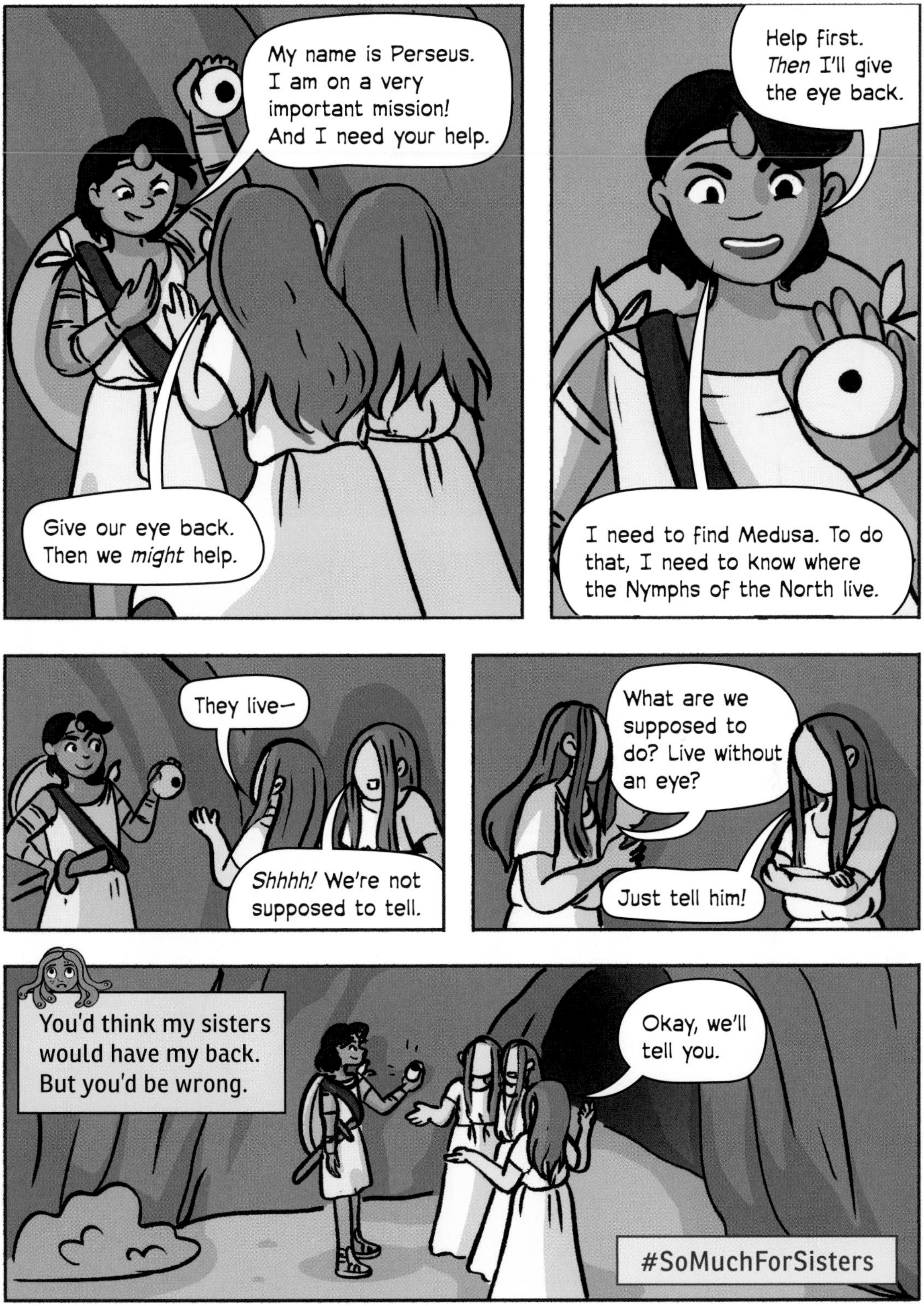
My name is Perseus. I am on a very important mission! And I need your help.
Give our eye back. Then we *might* help.
Help first. *Then* I'll give the eye back.
I need to find Medusa. To do that, I need to know where the Nymphs of the North live.
They live—
Shhhh! We're not supposed to tell.
What are we supposed to do? Live without an eye?
Just tell him!
You'd think my sisters would have my back. But you'd be wrong.
Okay, we'll tell you.
#SoMuchForSisters

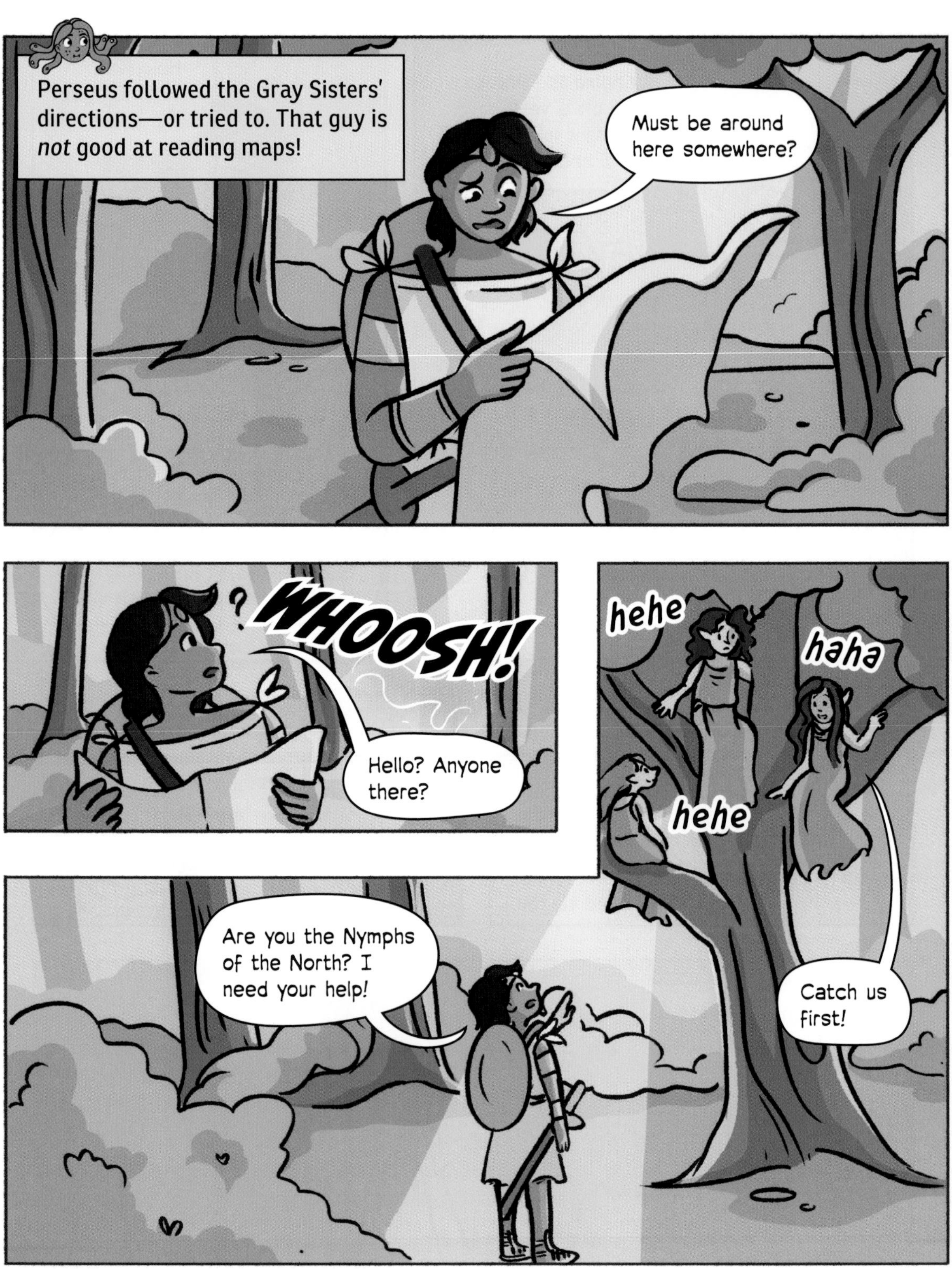
Perseus followed the Gray Sisters' directions—or tried to. That guy is *not* good at reading maps!
Must be around here somewhere?
?
WHOOSH!
Hello? Anyone there?
hehe
haha
hehe
Are you the Nymphs of the North? I need your help!
Catch us first!

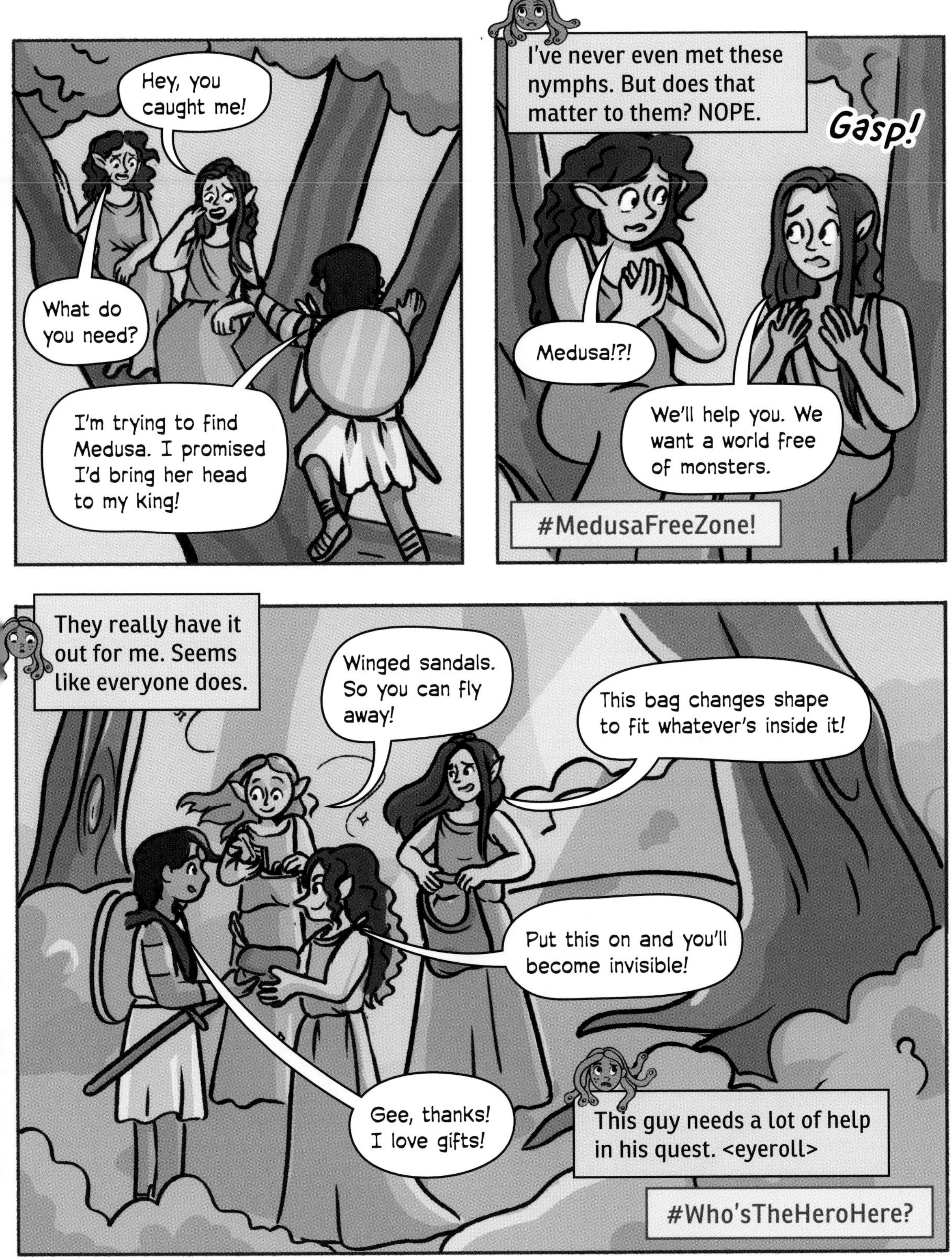
Hey, you caught me!
What do you need?
I'm trying to find Medusa. I promised I'd bring her head to my King!
I've never even met these nymphs. But does that matter to them? NOPE.
Gasp!
Medusa!?!
We'll help you. We want a world free of monsters.
#MedusaFreeZone!
They really have it out for me. Seems like everyone does.
Winged sandals. So you can fly away!
This bag changes shape to fit whatever's inside it!
Put this on and you'll become invisible!
Gee, thanks! I love gifts!
This guy needs a lot of help in his quest. <eyeroll>
#Who'sTheHeroHere?

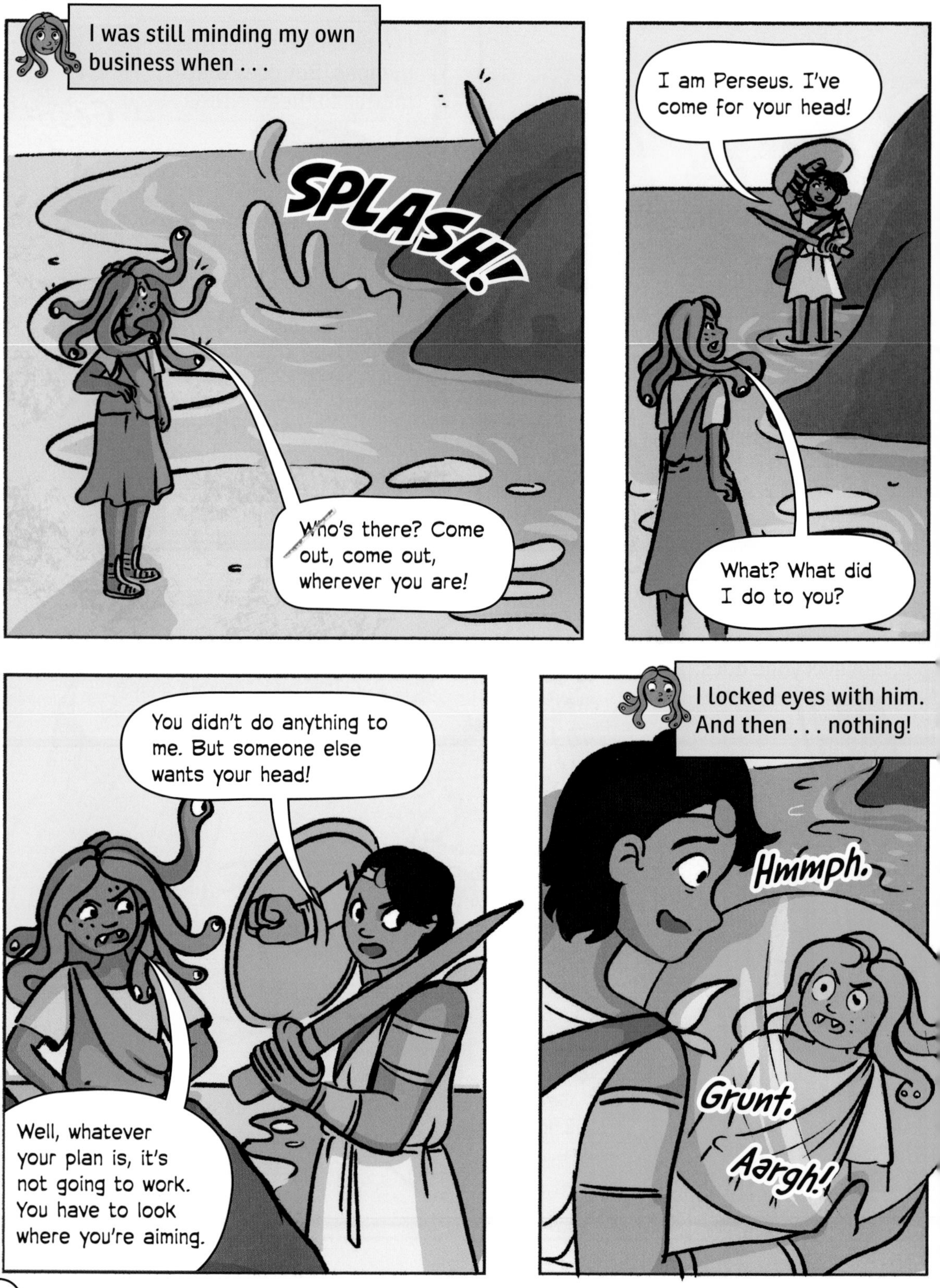
I was still minding my own business when . . .
SPLASH!
Who's there? Come out, come out, wherever you are!
I am Perseus. I've come for your head!
What? What did I do to you?
You didn't do anything to me. But someone else wants your head!
Well, whatever your plan is, it's not going to work. You have to look where you're aiming.
I locked eyes with him. And then . . . nothing!
Hmmph.
Grunt.
Aargh!

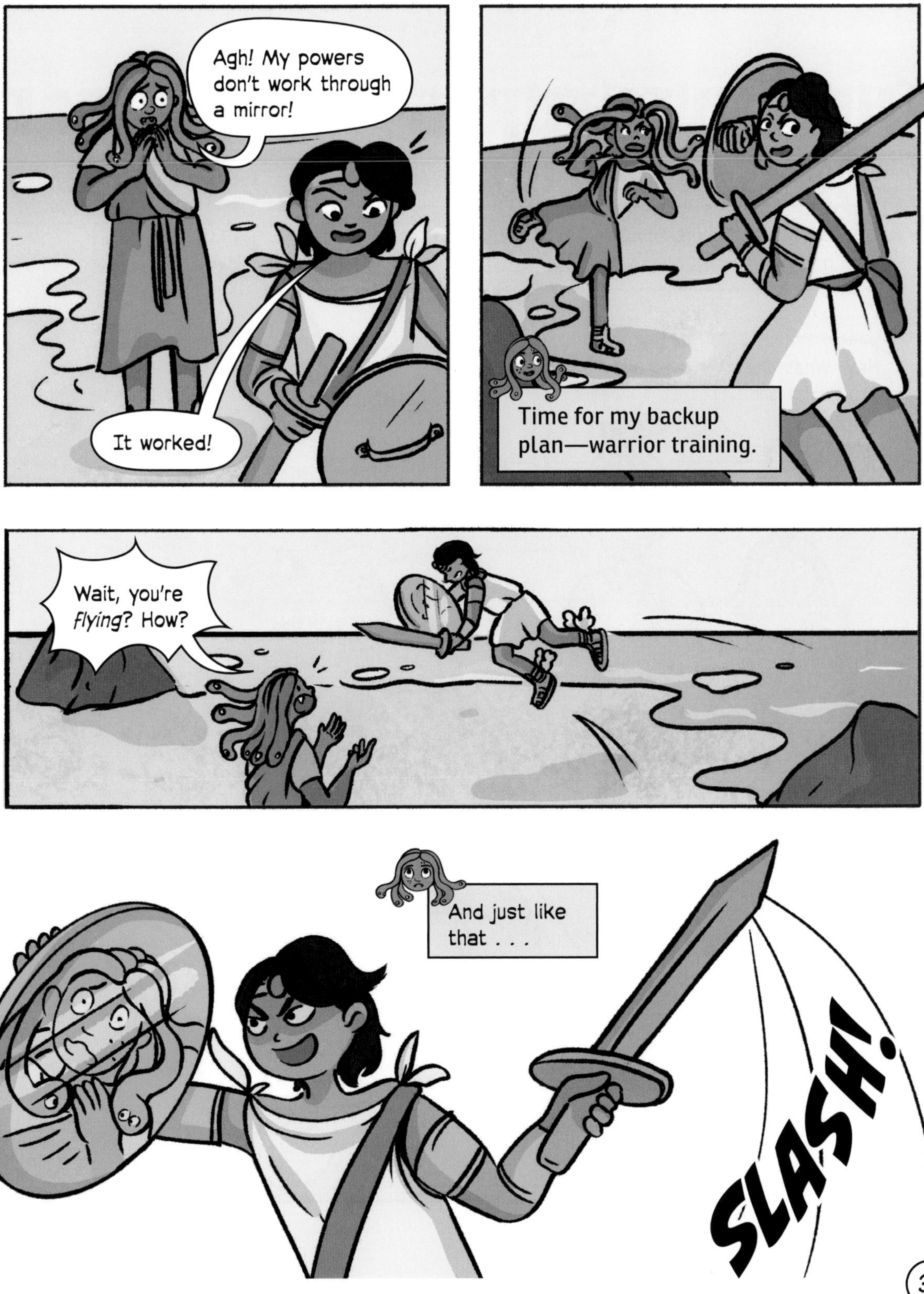
Agh! My powers don't work through a mirror!
It worked!
Time for my backup plan—warrior training.
Wait, you're *flying*? How?
And just like that . . .
SLASH!

CHAPTER 4

THE ADVENTURES OF MY HEAD

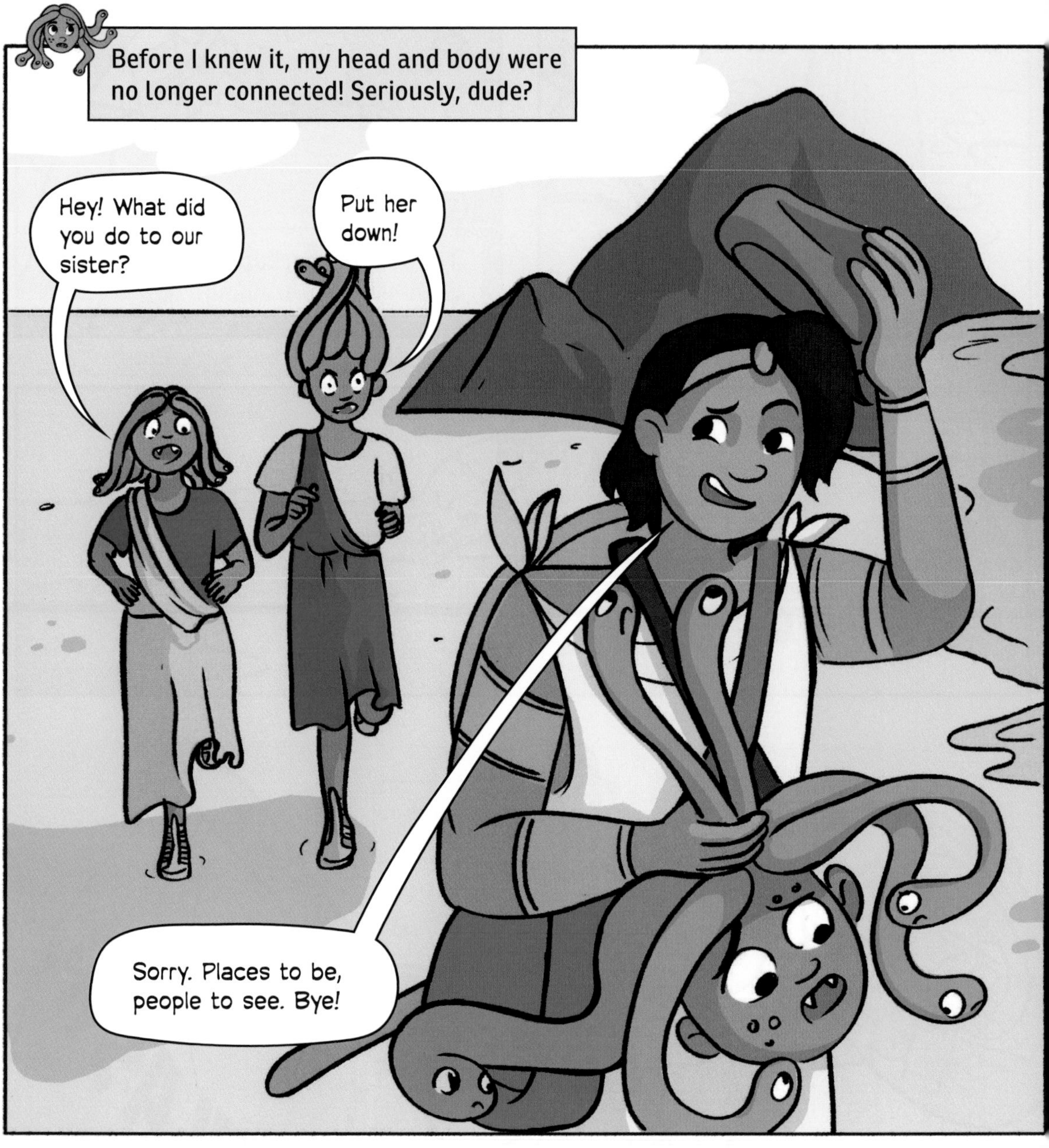
Before I knew it, my head and body were no longer connected! Seriously, dude?
Hey! What did you do to our sister?
Put her down!
Sorry. Places to be, people to see. Bye!

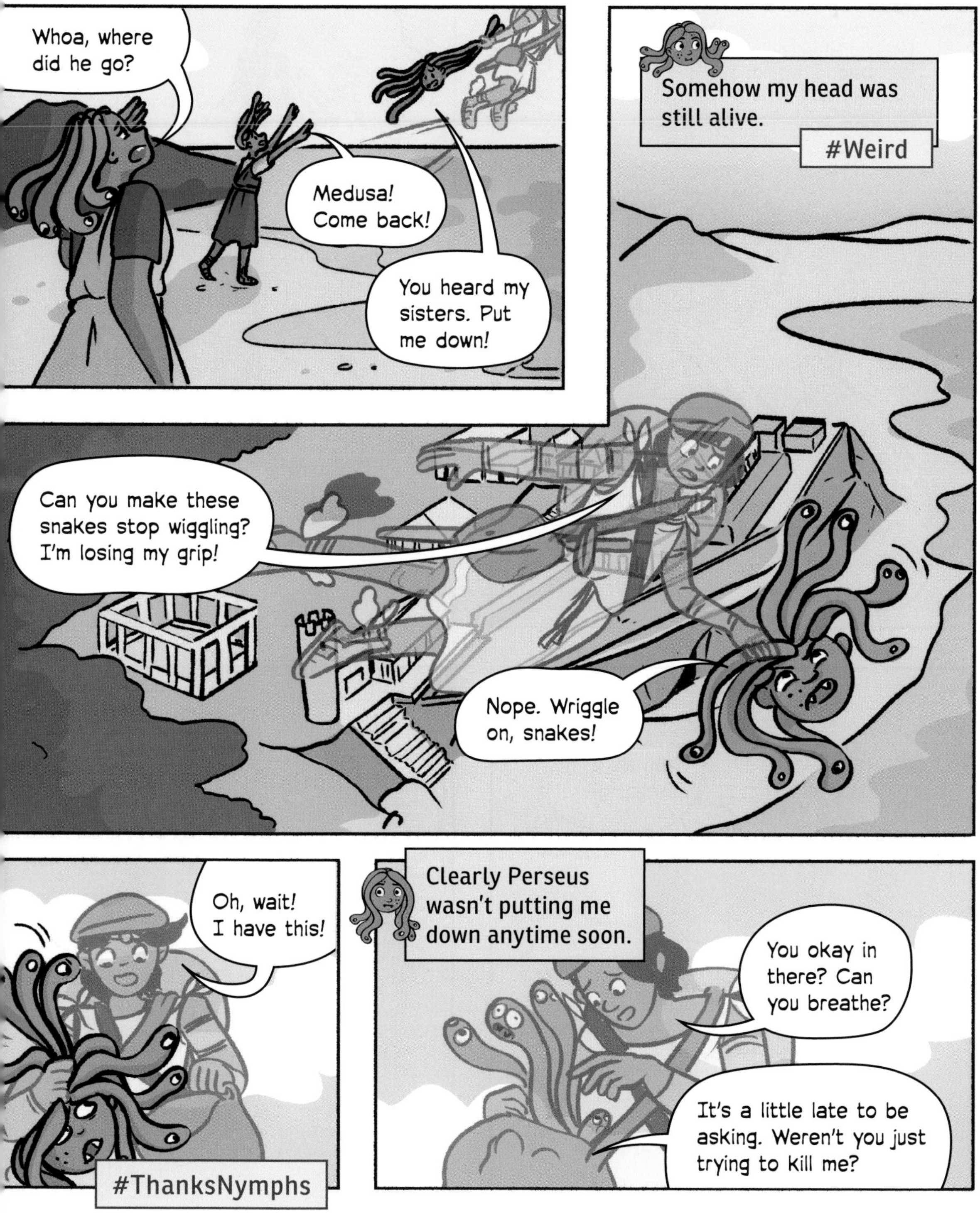

Whoa, where did he go?
Medusa! Come back!
You heard my sisters. Put me down!
Somehow my head was still alive.
#Weird
Can you make these snakes stop wiggling? I'm losing my grip!
Nope. Wriggle on, snakes!
Oh, wait! I have this!
#ThanksNymphs
Clearly Perseus wasn't putting me down anytime soon.
You okay in there? Can you breathe?
It's a little late to be asking. Weren't you just trying to kill me?

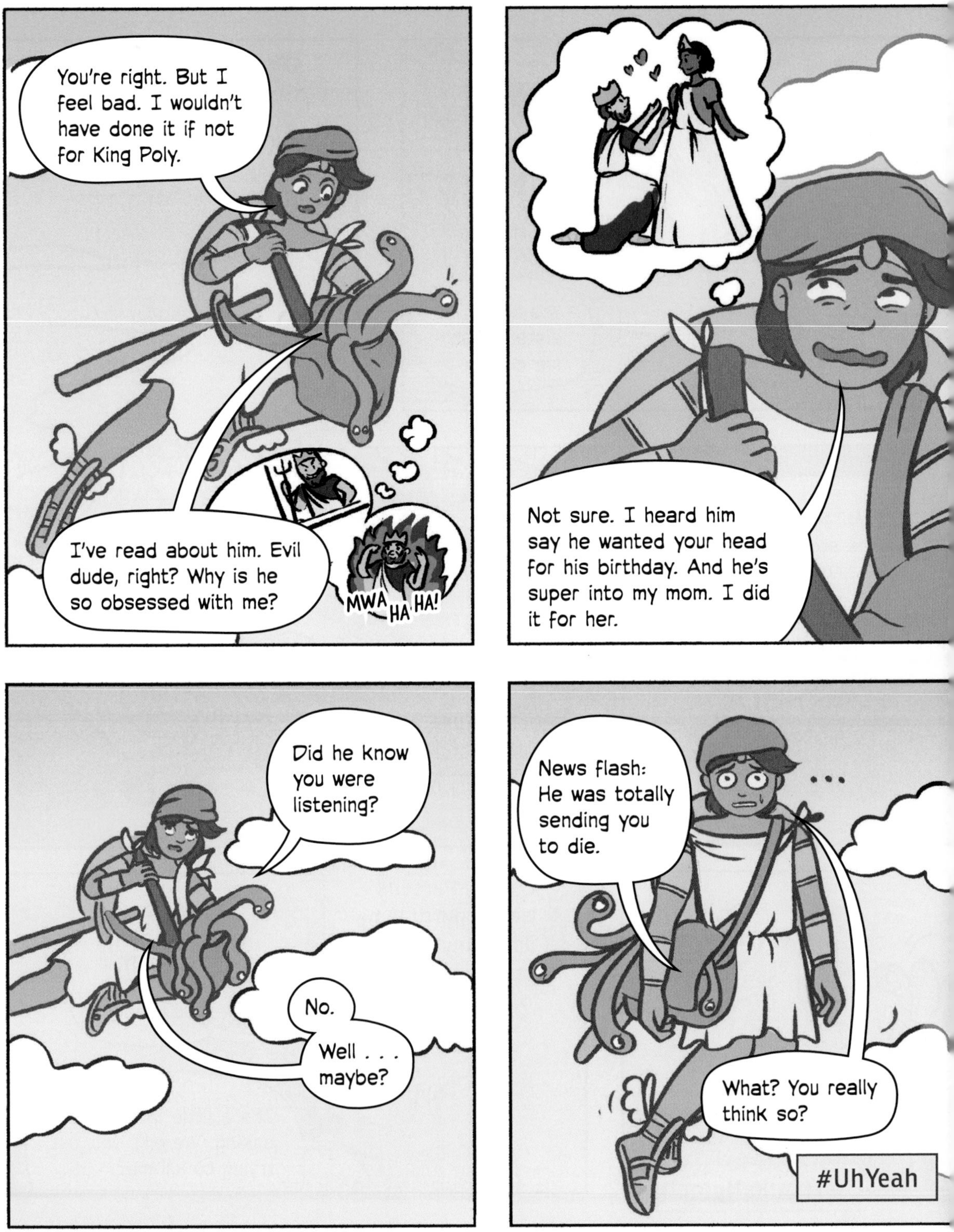

You're right. But I feel bad. I wouldn't have done it if not for King Poly.
I've read about him. Evil dude, right? Why is he so obsessed with me?
MWA HA HA!
Not sure. I heard him say he wanted your head for his birthday. And he's super into my mom. I did it for her.
Did he know you were listening?
No.
Well . . . maybe?
News flash: He was totally sending you to die.
. . .
What? You really think so?
#UhYeah

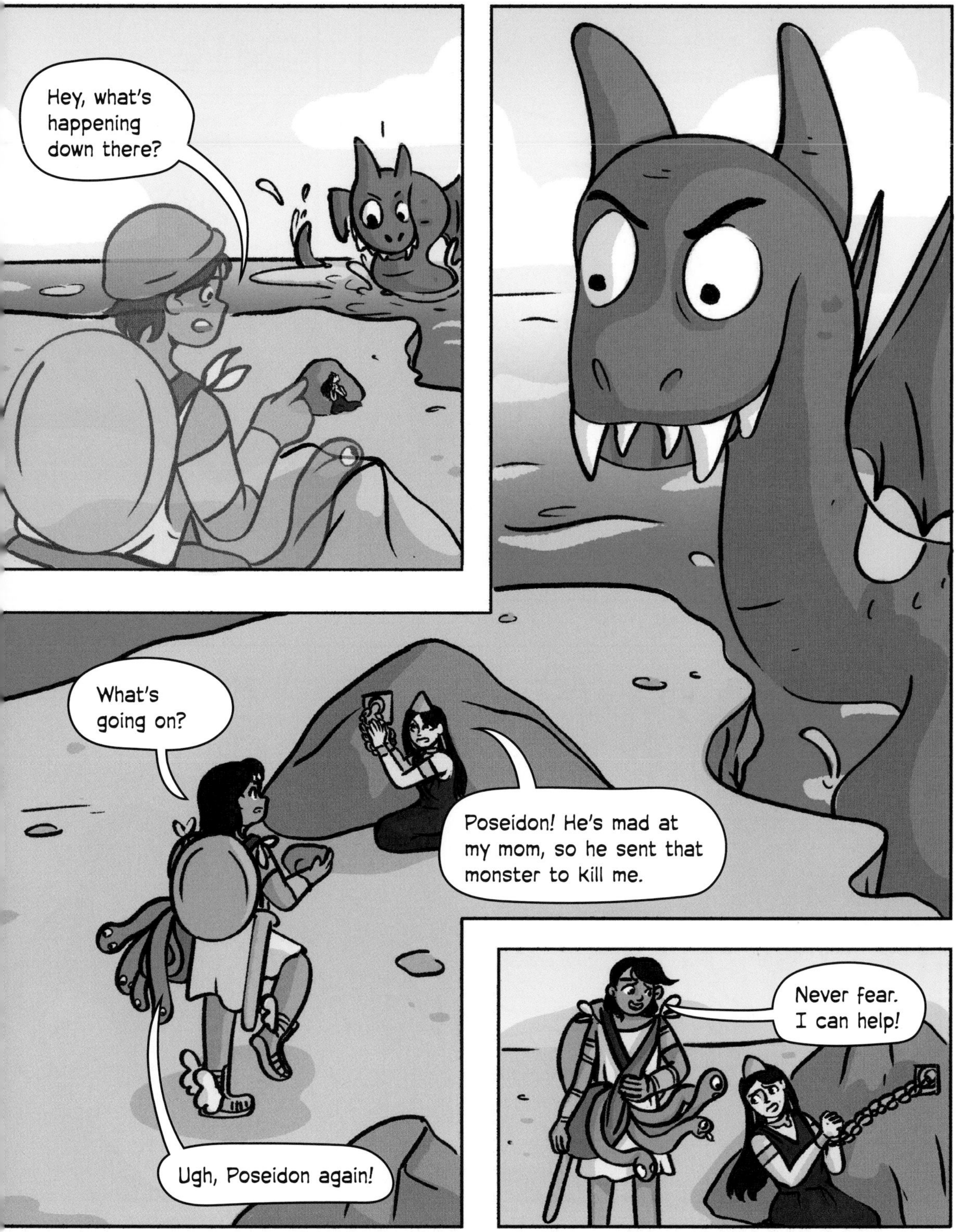
Hey, what's happening down there?
What's going on?
Poseidon! He's mad at my mom, so he sent that monster to kill me.
Ugh, Poseidon again!
Never fear. I can help!

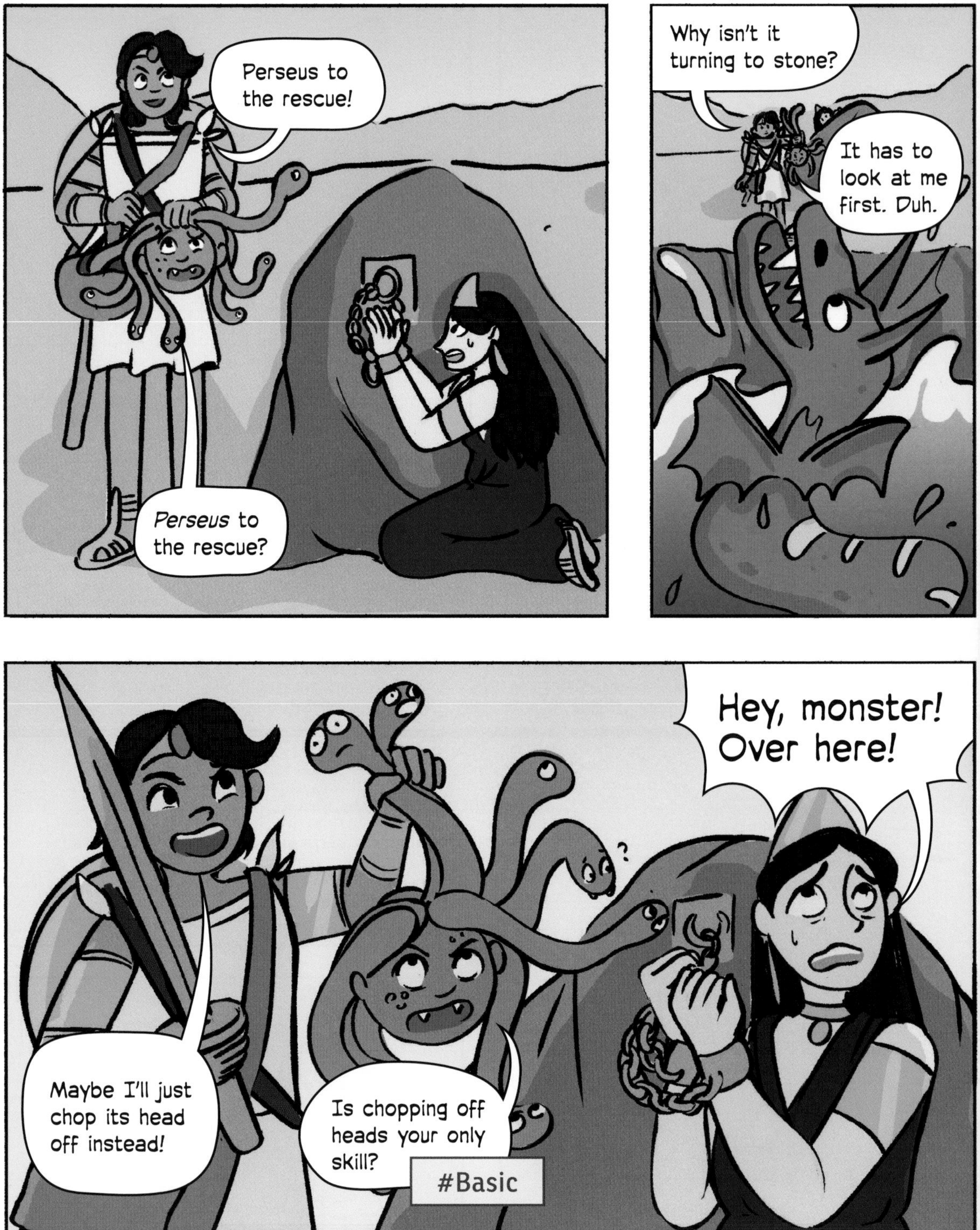

Perseus to the rescue!
Perseus to the rescue?
Why isn't it turning to stone?
It has to look at me first. Duh.
Hey, monster! Over here!
Maybe I'll just chop its head off instead!
Is chopping off heads your only skill?
#Basic

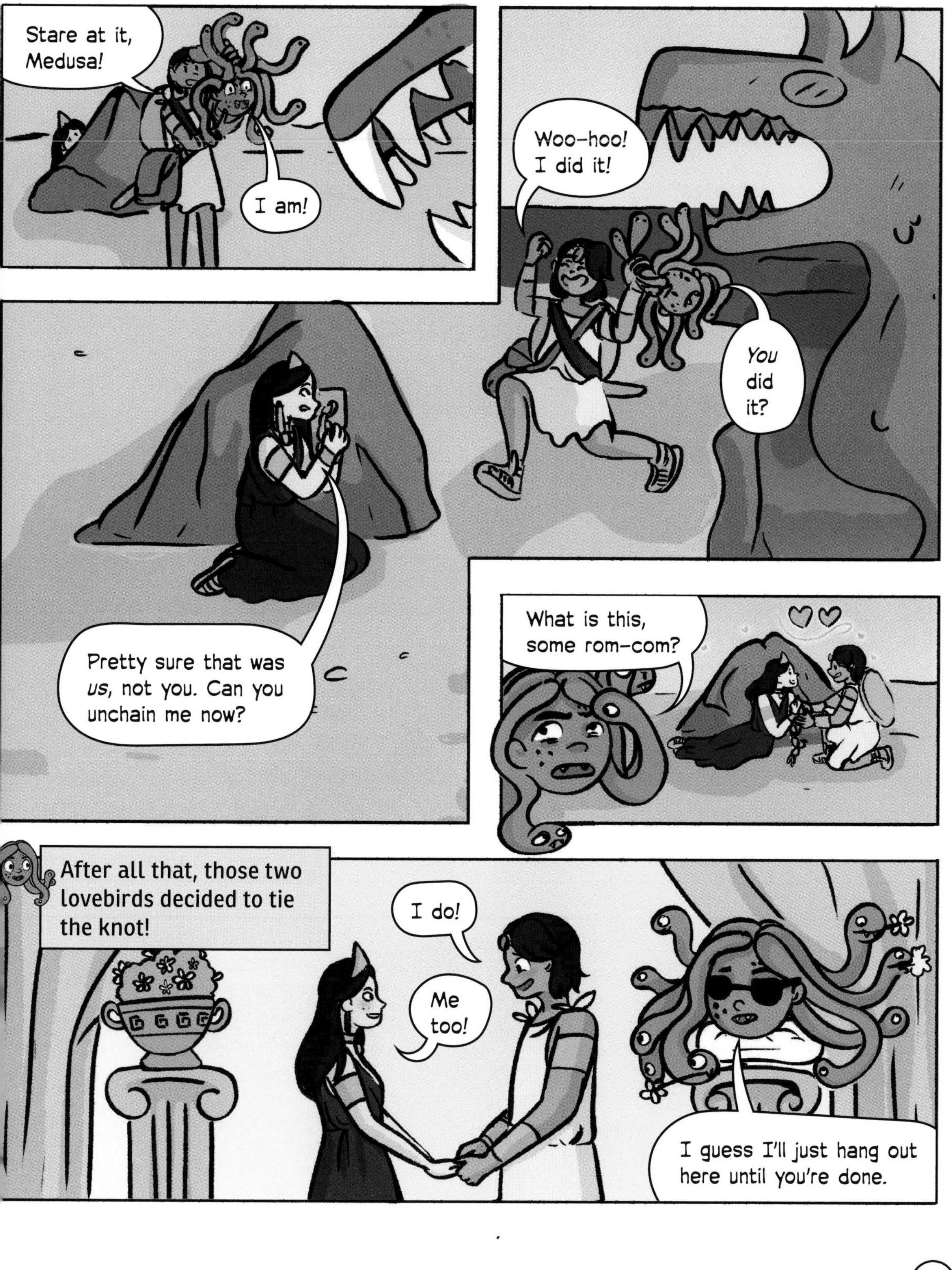
Stare at it, Medusa!
I am!
Woo-hoo! I did it!
You did it?
Pretty sure that was *us*, not you. Can you unchain me now?
What is this, some rom-com?
After all that, those two lovebirds decided to tie the knot!
I do!
Me too!
I guess I'll just hang out here until you're done.

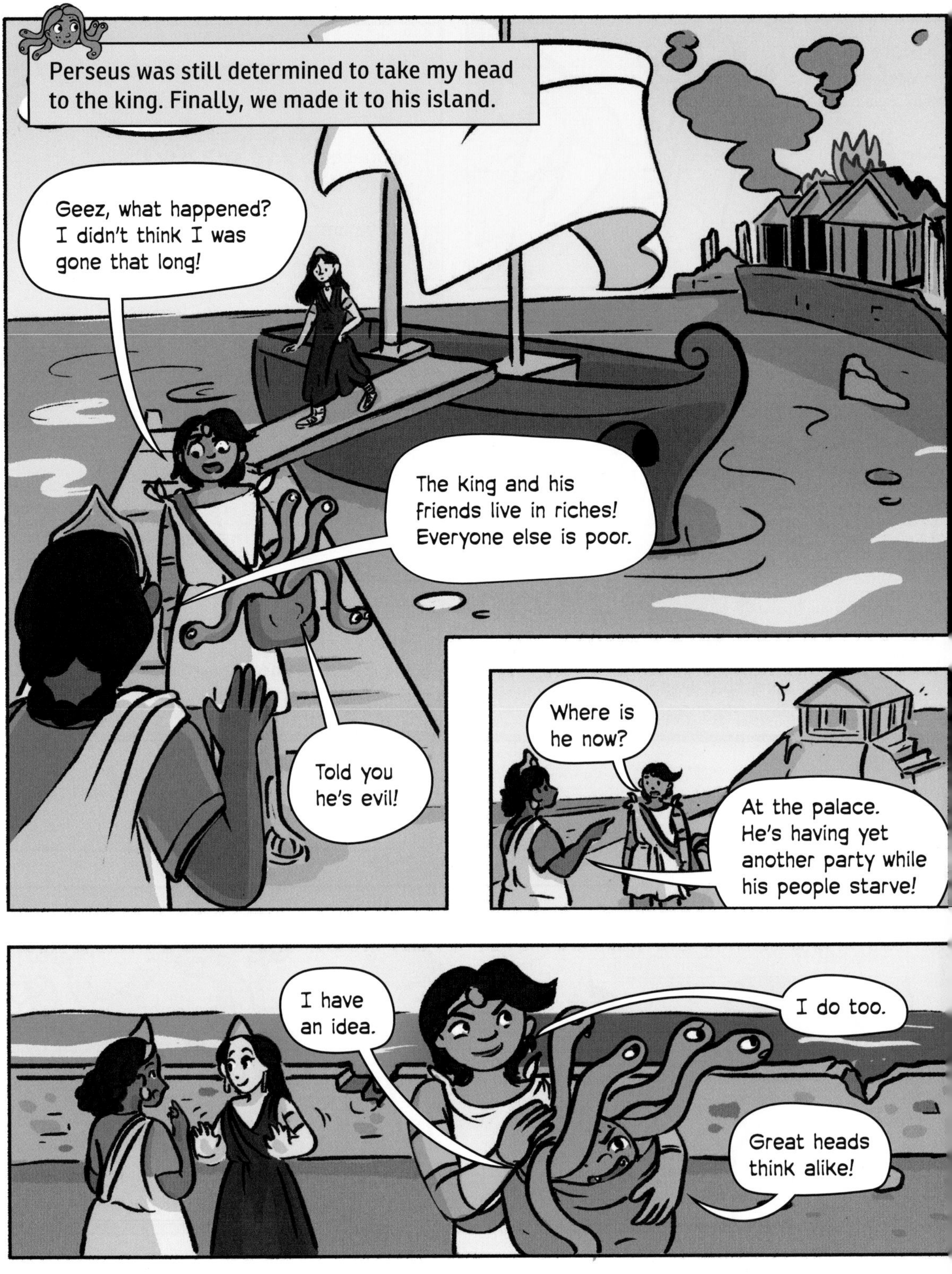
Perseus was still determined to take my head to the king. Finally, we made it to his island.
Geez, what happened? I didn't think I was gone that long!
The king and his friends live in riches! Everyone else is poor.
Told you he's evil!
Where is he now?
At the palace. He's having yet another party while his people starve!
I have an idea.
I do too.
Great heads think alike!

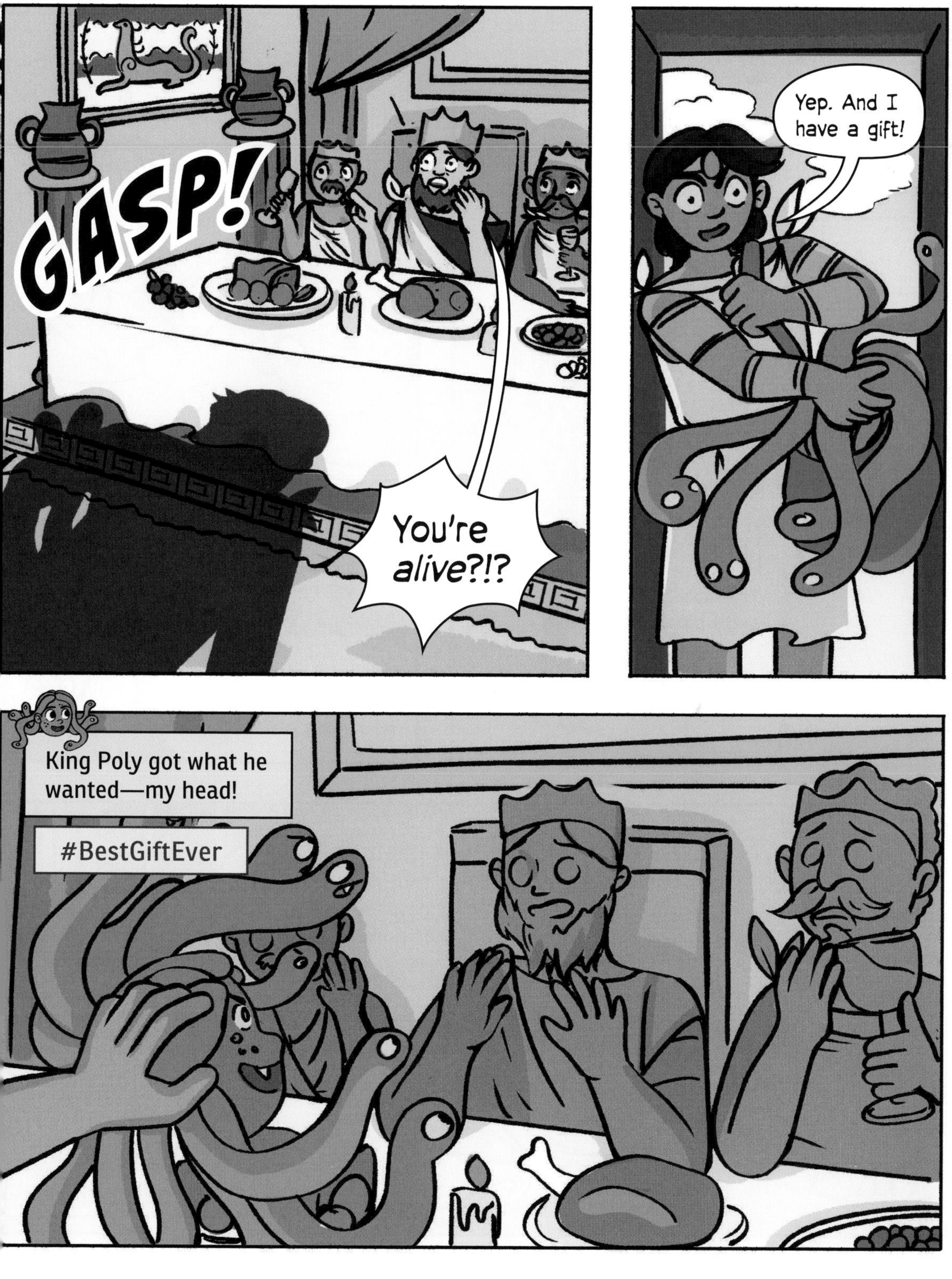
GASP!
You're *alive*?!?
Yep. And I have a gift!
King Poly got what he wanted—my head!
#BestGiftEver

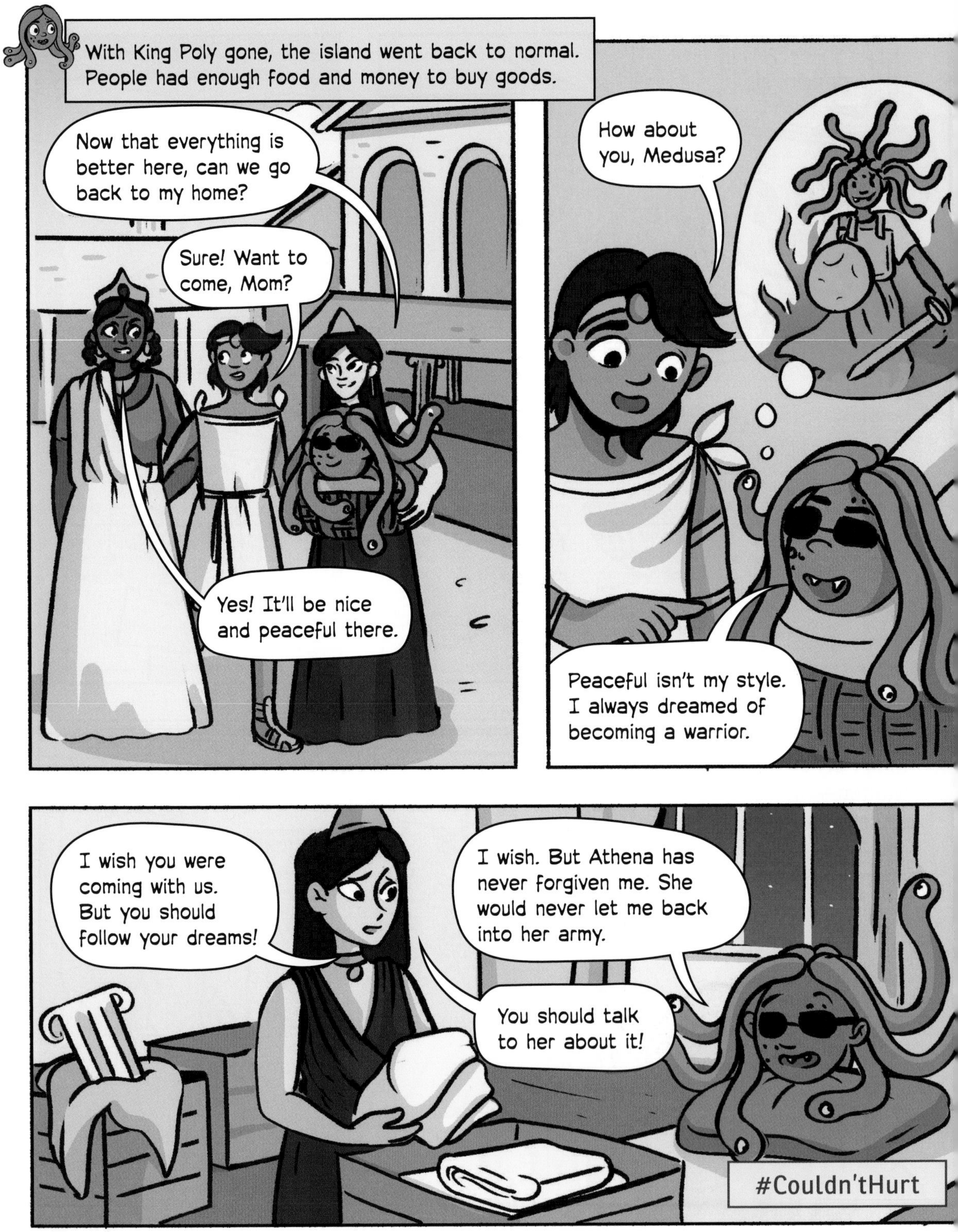
With King Poly gone, the island went back to normal. People had enough food and money to buy goods.
Now that everything is better here, can we go back to my home?
Sure! Want to come, Mom?
Yes! It'll be nice and peaceful there.
How about you, Medusa?
Peaceful isn't my style. I always dreamed of becoming a warrior.
I wish you were coming with us. But you should follow your dreams!
I wish. But Athena has never forgiven me. She would never let me back into her army.
You should talk to her about it!
#Couldn'tHurt

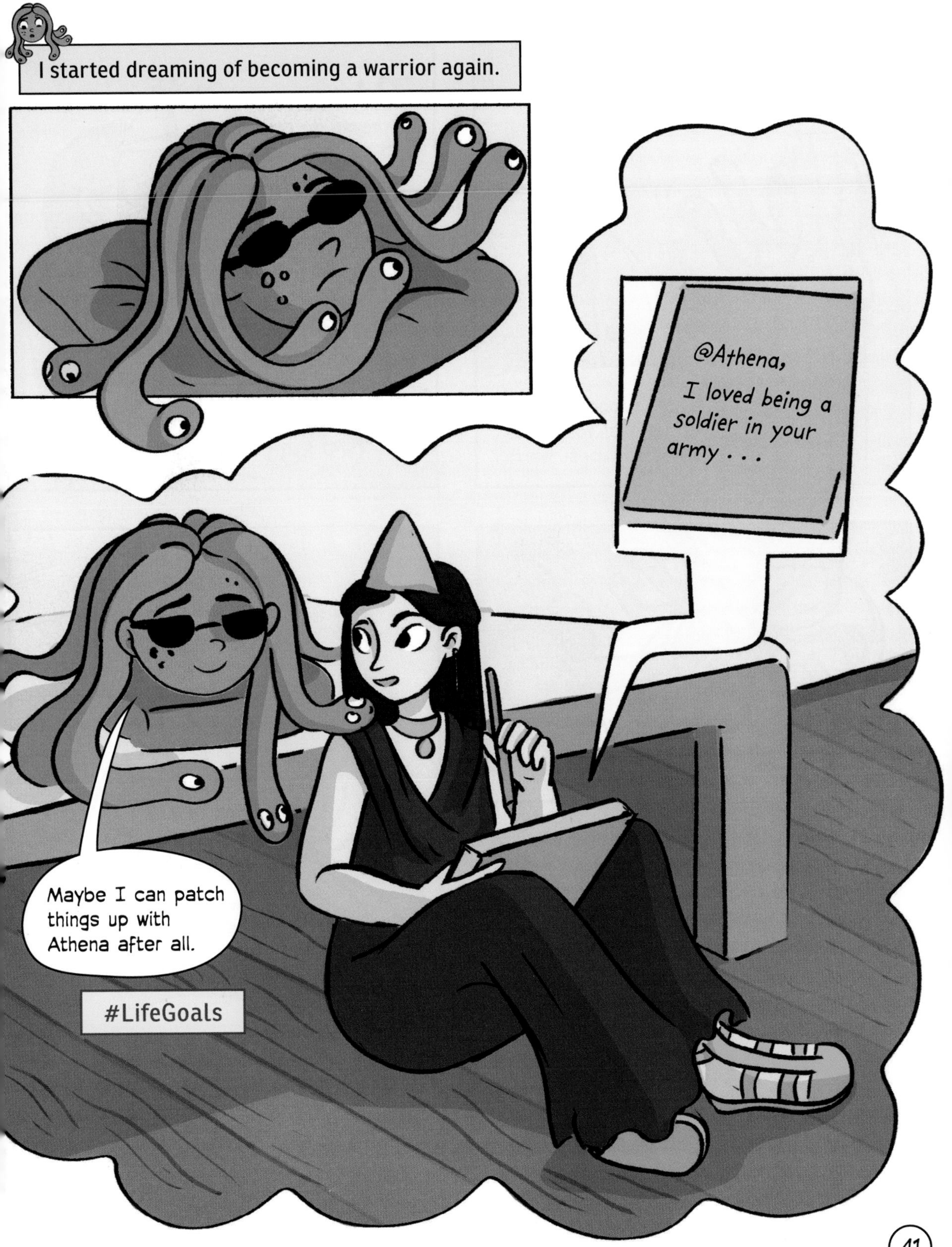
I started dreaming of becoming a warrior again.
@Athena,
I loved being a soldier in your army . . .
Maybe I can patch things up with Athena after all.
#LifeGoals

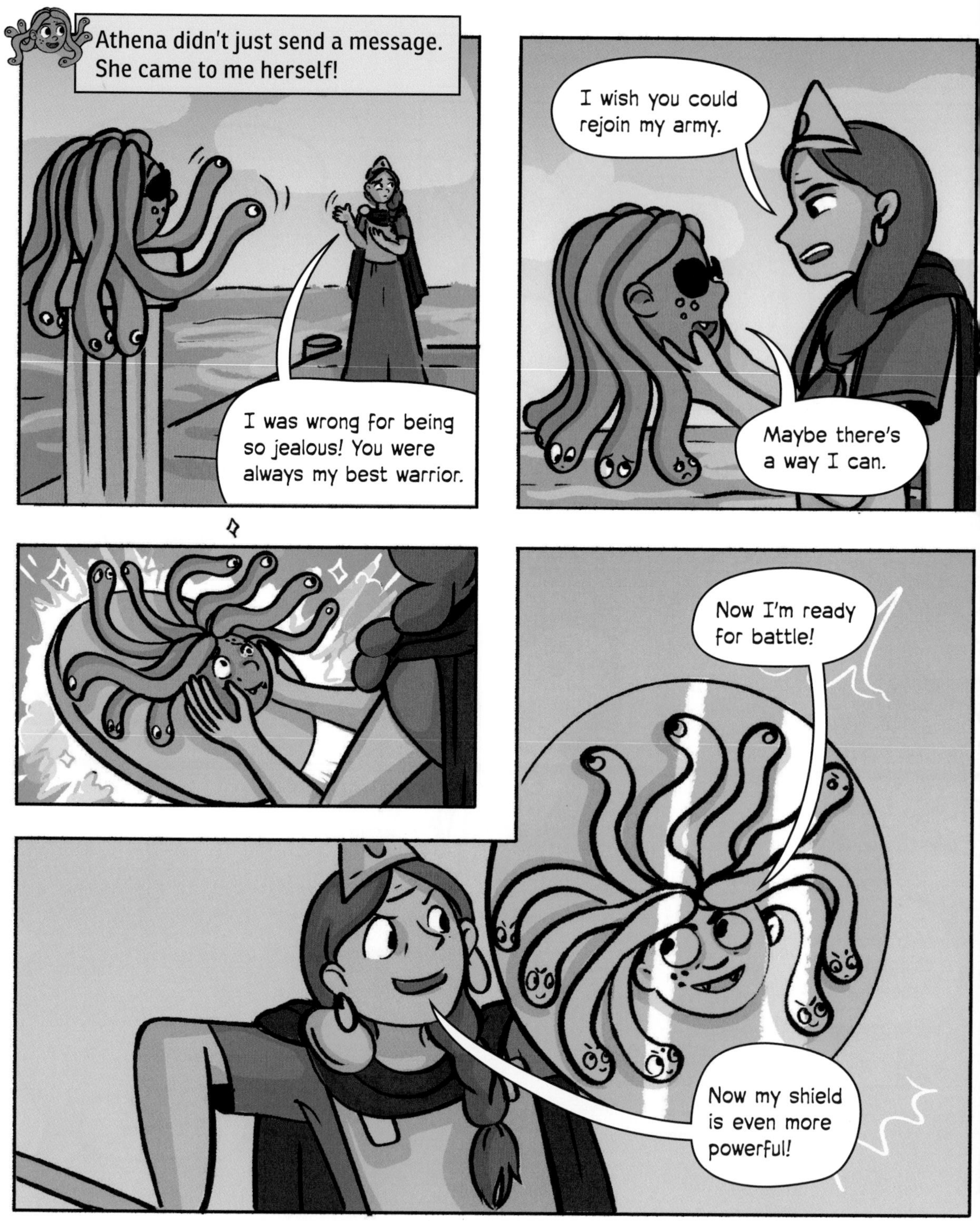
Athena didn't just send a message. She came to me herself!
I was wrong for being so jealous! You were always my best warrior.
I wish you could rejoin my army.
Maybe there's a way I can.
Now I'm ready for battle!
Now my shield is even more powerful!

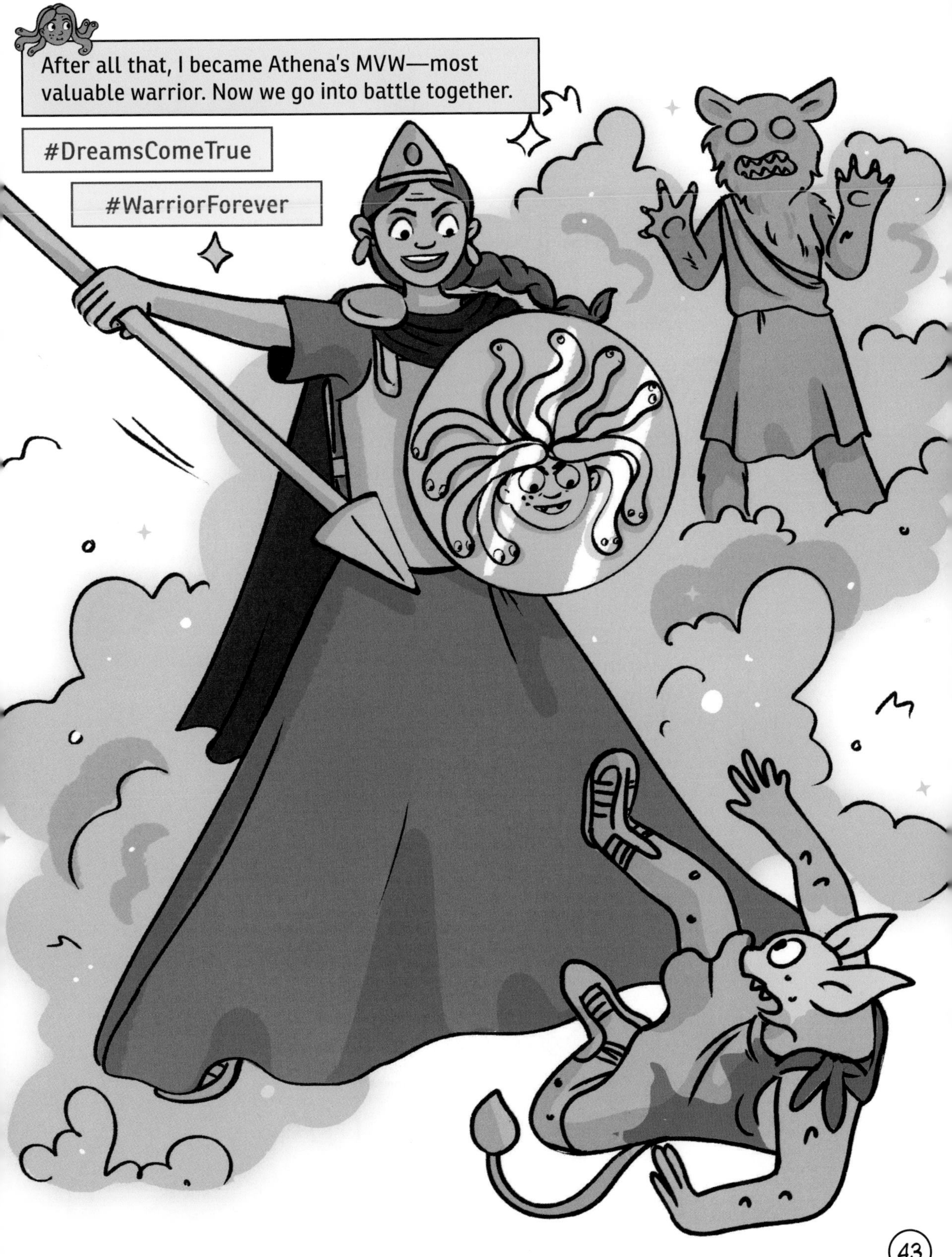
After all that, I became Athena's MVW—most valuable warrior. Now we go into battle together.
#DreamsComeTrue
#WarriorForever

More About Medusa

Another hero, Heracles, took a snake from Medusa's head. He used it to protect the town of Tegea from attack. The snake could cause a storm, which made enemies flee.

In some stories, two full-grown children spring from Medusa after she's killed. One is Pegasus, a winged horse. The other is Chrysaor, a giant with a golden sword.

In some versions of the myth, Medusa and her Gorgon sisters are not cursed by Athena. Instead, they are born as monsters.

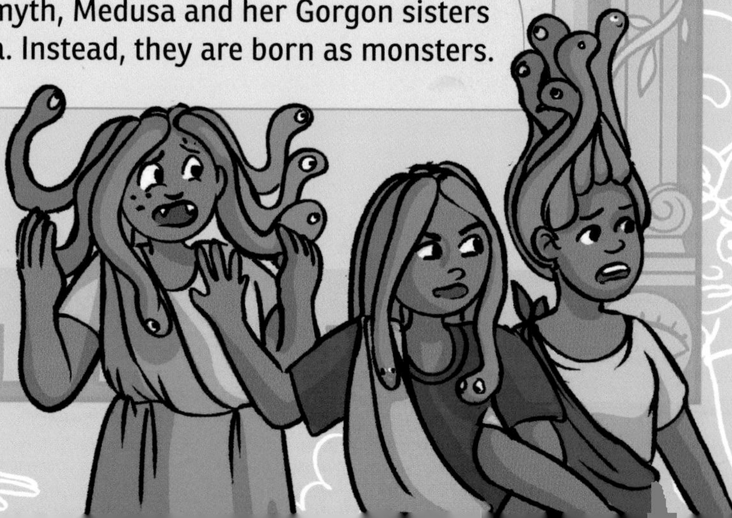

Some stories and artwork show Medusa having wings. Others show her with scales and claws.

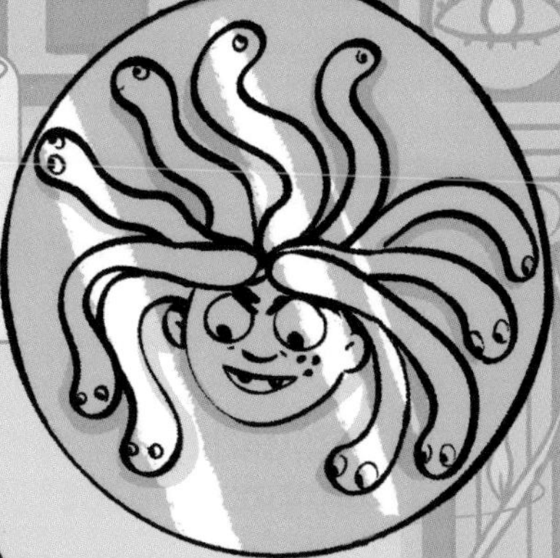

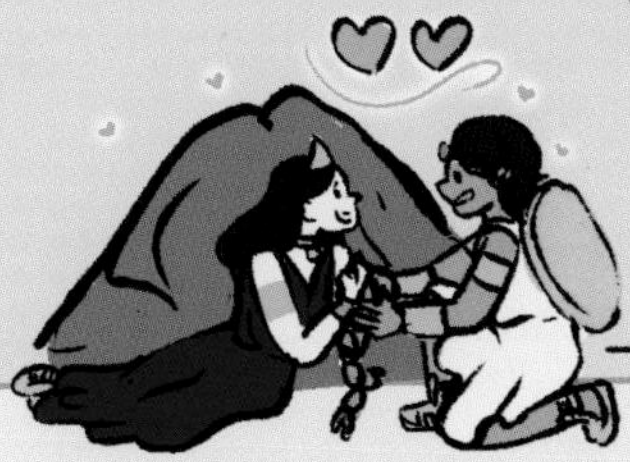

Perseus, his wife, Andromeda, and the sea monster that attacked her are all constellations in the night sky. Andromeda's mother, Cassiopeia, is also a constellation.

Many statues and artworks show Perseus holding Medusa's head. In 2020, a statue of Medusa holding Perseus's head was unveiled near a courthouse in New York City.

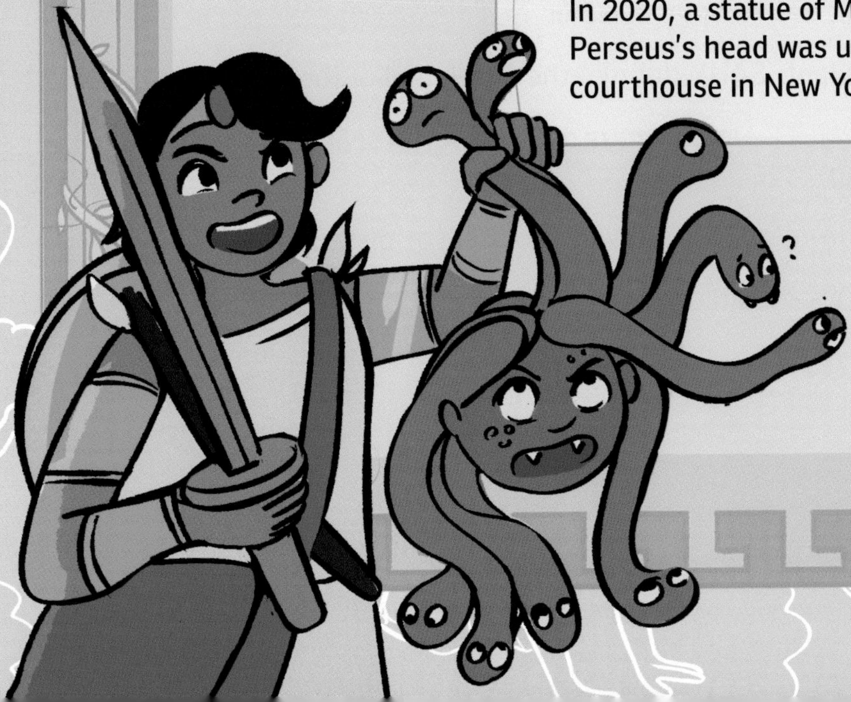

GLOSSARY

Athena (uh-THEE-nuh)—the Greek goddess of wisdom

constellation (kahn-stuh-LAY-shuhn)—a group of stars that forms a shape

Gorgon (GAWR-guhn)—any of three snaky-haired sisters in Greek mythology capable of turning anyone who looked at them to stone

grudge (GRUHJ)—a deep-seated resentment or ill will

immortal (ih-MOR-tuhl)—able to live forever

mortal (MOR-tuhl)—human, referring to a being who will eventually die

myth (MITH)—a story from ancient times

nymph (NIMF)—a mythical maiden on a mountain, in a forest, or in a body of water

Poseidon (poh-SAHY-duhn)—the Greek god of the sea

quest (KWEST)—an adventurous journey in search of something

remote (rih-MOHT)—far away, isolated, or distant

slay (SLEY)—to kill